STUDIES IN
MAJOR LITERARY
AUTHORS

T0270643

edited by
WILLIAM CAIN
WELLESLEY COLLEGE

THE PUSHER AND THE SUFFERER

An Unsentimental Reading of Moby-Dick

Suzanne Stein

Routledge
Taylor & Francis Group
New York   London

First published in 2000 by
Garland Publishing, Inc.

This edition published 2013 by Routledge

Routledge
Taylor & Francis Group
711 Third Avenue
New York, NY 10017

Routledge
Taylor & Francis Group
2 Park Square, Milton Park,
Abingdon, Oxfordshire OX14 4RN

First issued in paperback 2014

Routledge is an imprint of the Taylor & Francis Group, an informa business

Library of Congress Cataloging-in-Publication Data
Stein, Suzanne.
    The pusher and the sufferer : an unsentimental reading of
Moby Dick / Suzanne Stein.
        p. cm.— (Studies in major literary authors)
    Includes bibliographical references (p.) and index.
    ISBN 0-8153-3959-3 (alk. paper)
    1. Melville, Herman, 1819–1891. Moby Dick. 2. Sea stories, American—History and criticism. 3. Whaling in literature. 4. Whales in literature. I. Title. II. Series.
PS2384.M62 S685 2000
813'.3—dc21
                                                              00-044236

ISBN 13: 978-1-138-87845-7 (pbk)
ISBN 13: 978-0-8153-3959-5 (hbk)

For Ruth

The pusher and the sufferer will flock around the genital character to learn how to be like him. From this first impulse of the armor-ridden to emulate the freely-functioning Christ, the tragedy ensues with steel-like logic.

Wilheim Reich, The Murder of Christ

And as one who is sick and cannot move because he feels pain everywhere, and as one who is sick and cannot keep from moving as long as he lives, although he feels pain everywhere—so the religious individual lies fettered in the finite with the absolute conception of God present to him in human folly.

Kierkegaard, Postscript

Table of Contents

Introduction
Uses of Mendacity

Some years ago journalist Bill Moyers produced and P.B.S. aired a program about the late eighteenth-century hymn, "Amazing Grace," written by an Englishman who, after growing wealthy in the slave trade, looked at what he was doing and changed his life. During the program, Moyers interviewed the country singer, Johnny Cash, who remarked of the hymn that it is "a song without guile." I was sweeping at the time, and remember stopping in my tracks and looking at the television screen, at Cash's unusual face, the face of someone who, I had the impression, had lived deeply. As I remember, Cash sang his rendition of the hymn, then spoke more, very little. In what he did say, he seemed to distinguish between craft, the craft of making art, including a quality of shaping material so that an audience finds it evocative, and guile, a quality of deception. His observation struck me as one of the more astute, penetrating commentaries on aesthetics I had ever heard.

The other commentary on aesthetics apposite to my study of *Moby-Dick* is from an essay by Peter Gay, excerpts of which appeared in *Vogue* magazine in February, 1983, in celebration of the Metropolitan Opera and Patrice Chereau's production of Wagner's *Ring*. Gay discusses the primitivism, exoticism and febrile heroism associated with Wagner's operas, and the composer's explicit intention in his staging and costuming, as well as score, of imparting to the audience a sense that they, along with the characters, are larger than life. (Melville scholar James Baird, writing of ritualized "primitive religious acts(s)" that characterize the "natu-

ral hero," makes a similar point regarding Wagner, and draws
comparisons between Pierre and Siegfried.[1]) The "elevated condition" into which numerous Wagner admirers, Bruno Walter for
one, have claimed to be transported, and Wagner's instinct for
"...[giving] his public what it want[s] without making it feel too
guilty" account for much of his appeal, Gay suggests, and accounts
also for the repugnance—Nietzsche eventually felt sickened—
expressed by other listeners (ms.). Gay is citing a letter written by
one Elizabet von Herzogenberg, a "talented amateur musician and
close friend of Brahms," (ms.) who attended a performance of
Parsifal at Bayreuth and was appalled, not many years after Mark
Twain had visited and evinced his own bemused astonishment at
the spectacle there, off the stage and on. "...this table," von
Herzogenberg begins her letter, "has not been set for us:"

> She had just come from the Bayreuth festival and sat down to
> compose a splendid diatribe to friends. She was pleased to
> have experienced Bayreuth, she said, at long last. "It has
> strengthened us marvelously." "Never," she added, had she
> and her husband "felt more clearly than we do now why we
> resist this art...Let those who lie to themselves," and here she
> lists Herman Levi and other furious Wagnerites, "let them to
> whom this indeed has become a sacred thing and who have
> long since ceased to be able to distinguish gluttony from
> esthetic enjoyment, let them sit down at the table and
> carouse. For those devout diners gorging themselves, it was a
> holy feast...Oh, I tell you," she wrote, getting angrier and
> angrier by the minute, "I tell you the whole business smells
> really very bad, like a church that has never been aired, or a
> butcher stall in summer. There is a bloodthirstiness and
> incense snuffing, a sultry sensuality with holy and solemn ges-
> tures, a heaviness and bombast unknown to all other art. In
> conclusion, *Parsifal* is nothing but sensuality, the sloppiest
> emotional debauchery and unhealthiest stigmata ecstasy. For
> a stomach accustomed to a diet of Bach, it is almost emetic
> (Gay, *Vogue*, February, 1983, p. 346).

The pertinence of Cash's and von Herzogenberg's remarks, of
emotional debauchery, stigmata ecstasy, churches never aired, and
bloodthirstiness accompanied by holy, grandiose and absurdly
solemn gestures will become clear in coming pages, for my study
of *Moby-Dick* is a consideration of aesthetics, in the same sense
that the country singer and classical musician are, in their disparate fashions, considering aesthetics. In this respect it differs rad-
ically from the main currents of Melville scholarship, which in this

Introduction I will broadly characterize as comprising two periods, or schools, each represented in biographical studies published in 1996: Laurie Robertson-Lorant's *Melville: A Biography*, Hershel Parker's *Herman Melville: A Biography*, and Elizabeth Renker's *Strike Through the Mask: Herman Melville and the Scene of Writing*, and two comprehensive critical anthologies: *A Companion to Melville Studies*, published in 1986, edited by John Bryant, and *The Cambridge Companion to Herman Melville*, published in 1998, edited by Robert Levine. I mean to draw the general parameters of the two schools in the following discussion, focussing on those scholarly conversations about *Moby-Dick* to which my study responds. This should orient the reader to how my approach differs.

It may be helpful that I mention now at the outset that as I have grown older, my understanding of Melville's work and the scholarship it inspires has materially changed. In my twenties, when I read *Moby-Dick* seriously for the first time, I felt again the excitement of the novel that I had felt at thirteen. I was also aware of feeling an unease I could not define, which for a long time I ignored. I was, still, as unable to entertain the thought that erudite brilliance such as Melville's might accompany a sensibility jejune, disingenuous and banal, than I could foretell how much my own taste would change.

* * * * *

Several contributors to the Bryant and Levine anthologies note the centrality of that amorphous thing, Romanticism, and the Romantic image of the artist, to Herman Melville's sensibility. It is a theme or sub-theme in the essays of Martin Bickman, Robert Milder, Brian Higgins and Hershel Parker, Shirley M. Dettlaff and Bette S. Weidman, whose remarks about Melville's earlier work apply as well to *Moby-Dick*: "The only perspective that is possible is that of the Romantic—'a meditative outsider who at the bottom of his heart does not know what world he belongs to.'"[2] The idea that Modernism, ostensibly so antipathetic to Romance, is rooted in Romantic thought, and is often another form of it, is addressed by Kingsley Widmer, who looks at how Melville, like other "nineteenth-century writer[s]...supplied..." and envisioned himself in his artistic vocation as supplier of "apocalyptic metaphors."[3] But Romanticism is central not only to Melville; it is also the heart of scholarship, old and new, about him. Bryant is echoing the earlier work of Walter Bezanson, and a train of scholarship Bezanson started, when he writes in his Introduction that "Melville the Ignored Artist is the dominant, romantic image of the man that has most captivated American scholars."[4]

I define the first period, or school, of Melville scholarship, then, as steeped in the High Romanticism inherited from Schiller, Schelling, Lessing and Goethe, adumbrated by Weaver, Willard Thorp and Charles Anderson, and sustained through the majority of subsequent textual as well as biographical studies, notably the work of Lawrence, Olson, Mumford, and, later, Gilman, Howard, Arvin, Chase, Levin and Fiedler. The first school includes what Levine, citing the Historical Note in the Northwestern-Newberry *Moby-Dick*, calls "the great generation of Melville researchers of the 1930's and 1940's,"[5] but also goes both forward in time to scholarship of the 1950's, and backward, to Lessing's *Laocoon*, Keats' letters, *Werther* and *Manfred*. An important nineteenth-century adherent of the first school is Melville himself, imagining the literary artist as a Daemon beset by daemons, who, while in the act of creating his art, becomes a metaphysically distinct order of being that bears no relation to who he is when he is performing other tasks—feeding the horse, for example. This is the specifically Romantic rendition of a Pindaric icon: the poet as hallowed, shamanic figure seized by the Muse, the poet's voice not his own but Hers, the poet's eyes, as Elizabethans will say a thousand years after Pindar, rolling in fine frenzy. The first school, and the second, tend to embrace Freud; as Eleanor Metcalf begins making available to early Melville scholars unlovely family anecdotes and letters about her grandfather, Herman Melville, the psychoanalytic approach to literary criticism is being born, and the history of Melville scholarship largely parallels the diffusion of Freudian thought, *The Interpretation of Dreams* especially, through American intellectual life. Forty years later, Freud, and a Freudian reading of the then still secret documents regarding Melville's domestic life, is the touchstone in the work of Henry Murray, who, according to Forrest G. Robinson in his biography of Murray, and Renker in her comments on the Robinson biography, felt a "'personal identification'" with Melville that "consumed" him (*Strike*, 54).

With few exceptions across the decades—Ludwig Lewisohn, Lawrance Thompson, Richard Blau, Donald Pease, William Spanos—consuming personal identification with Melville remains a defining feature of Melville studies, achieving its fullest expression in Parker's biography. In 1946 the Melville Society is born. Reflecting the overwhelming tenor of the scholarship, for the Melville Society, as for Parker—this is where my study diverges sharply from the first school—"Herman Melville is the hero."[6]

"Hero" is one the issues I will explore. In the second paragraph of his Introduction, Levine cites Emerson's famous warning about "the danger that the 'love of the hero' will become corrupted into the 'worship of his statue,'" and in the Afterword of the *Cambridge Companion*, Andrew Delbanco says that the essays there all "dissent from prevailing dogmas."[7] And certainly the essays in both *Companions* do, from many dogmas.

Not, however, from the dogma—Levine, a gentleman, calls dogmas "scholarly legends"—not from the scholarly legend that Ishmael is earnestly engaged in an "effort to know the whale."[8] Nor from the legend, propounded by Ishmael, that Ahab knows recondite truths known to few others, the legend that his "knowledge" is "tragic,"[9] the legend that he is "tragic,"[10] that he is "*post*-tragic,"[11] that he is an "Elizabethan tragic hero."[12] Much less do contributors dissent from the overarching legend that Melville, having "the Promethean perspective,"[13] being "'a godlike mind without a God,'"[14] possesses the sobriety, calm or *gravitas* of tragic vision.

Contributors to neither *Companion* ask whether it might be a legend, propounded by the narrator, that he is "saved from Ahab's soul-curdling bitterness,"[15] having "slip[ped] out from Ahab's hot hand:"[16] a fantastic, superbly-executed, specious legend that Ishmael, and behind him, Melville, is seriously engaged in the telling of "prophetic truths."[17]

Maybe I'm of that kind of Jewishness that, choose to or not, reads ultimately with the stomach, though some of the earlier, non-Jewish scholars like Lewisohn seem to do it too. However it may be, my experience of reading *Moby-Dick* belies the theories cited above, theories which constitute the foundation of contemporary Melville scholarship, which means that for me they are legends.

And if they are legends, the legends of the first school, Romantic to its marrow, they are, by and large, seamlessly incorporated into the second school, or period, developing in the wake of the 1960's. For the second school does not genuinely question the inherited icon of the demon-hero/hero-writer either, or question other Romantic tenets of earlier scholarship: the tenet that

Passion is finer than Reason, that loud noise multiplied by com-
plex syntax equals deep feeling, that suffering necessarily leads to
wisdom. Nor does it register awareness of the aggregated, increasing meaninglessness of its inherited idiom, an idiom whose hall-
mark is silly, if ponderous, pronouncement: Ahab is the "first modern hero;"[18] Ahab is a "hero-villain"[19] The biggest difference, in
fact, between earlier and more recent studies of Melville is that
newer scholarship, far from questioning the *idees fixe* of
Romanticism, refurbishes them by more vigorously, indiscrimi-
nately collapsing distinctions, as though such distinctions are
merely ornamental, between the concept of "hero"—Ishmael now,
along with Ahab, along with Melville—with "antihero."

Thus, supplementing the legends above, is the legend that
Ahab's "crazy logic" is synonymous with, and vaguely equivalent
to, a higher logic, a *"paralogic,"*[20] the repeat-legend that Melville
endows the *Pequod* crew with "'tragic graces,'"[21] the repeat-
repeat legend that *Moby-Dick* is a "cautionary tale" by egalitari-
an hero Melville-Ishmael about totalitarian antihero Melville-
Ahab.[22]

Confusion of hero with antihero, demonic with tragic, tragic
with psychopathic suffuses earlier scholarship; the work of Arvin
and Edinger are examples. But it also suffuses more recent work,
including that of Richard Brodhead, Sharon Cameron, William
Dillingham, and the *Companions*, whose studies tacitly accept the
assumption that, whatever else Melville may be doing in *Moby-
Dick*, he must surely, surely be critiquing Ahab.

What, though, if he isn't?

What if, as John Huston thought, "Ahab speaks for
Melville?"[23] *Speaks for Melville*, in a quite unequivocal fashion?

What if that is why the book is so exciting?

What if the excitement of the exciting story, told through
Ishmael about Ahab, is Ishmael's excitement?

Even a reader as comfortable with Ishmael as Bezanson
acknowledges that the narrator entertains a "half-secret admira-
tion" for Ahab, which he does "not entirely [hide]" from readers.[24] What if calling Ishmael's feelings about Ahab a "half" secret
makes as much sense as calling the other side of the half-moon a
"secret?" What if, as Huston thought, "The message of Moby
Dick [sic] was hate."[25] What if Ishmael is as thoroughly enchanted with Ahab and Ahab's hate as the thrill in his voice from the
beginning to the end of the novel demonstrates him to be? So

enchanted he can't see straight. Enchanted as a thirty-two year old man permanently arrested in a precocious, anguished adolescence can be, and stay, enchanted.

This possibility, simple, crass, discomfiting and obvious, has not been examined in a sustained manner, although it has tantalized many scholars. It haunts some, when they let themselves be haunted: Does hateful Ahab *speak for* Melville? (He can't possibly! Everlastingly No!) One whom it haunted half his natural life was Henry Murray, whose writings, along with those of David Leverenz and Sharon Cameron, are widely considered the best psychological criticism of Melville yet published.[26] Lawrance Thompson did wonder, out loud! if Ahab speaks for Melville, and if that is why Ishmael can't take his eyes off Ahab or stop talking about Ahab. By nineteenth-century reviewers, typically regarded today as naïve, this was not considered an impudent question, much less unaskable, but it has become so for us, because the accretion of academic legend on top of legend into virtual legend-strata, has just this effect. (See Johannes D. Bergmann's "Melville's Tales," where he alludes to "the American academic need simply to *produce* scholarship"[27]).

It has continued to tantalize, nonetheless, and the anti-authoritarian points of view of many writers in recent decades, especially Michael Paul Rogin, Robert Martin, Charles Haberstroh, Carolyn Porter and Judith Fetterley bring attention to important related issues, especially the issue of sadism, and the issue of the narrator's infatuation with the protagonist. The recent biographers, moreover, with their greater access to controversial archival material from the Shaw, Metcalf, Gansevoort and Melville families, also occasionally cross into the dimension of inquiry my study proposes, which I will briefly address now.

In one aspect of Renker's work, her speculations about Melville's embattled relationship to the empty white page, on the one hand, and to other people, especially his family, on the other, my reading coincides with hers. It coincides also with Robertson-Lorant's understanding of the traumas of Melville's childhood, his extraordinary sensitivity and what befell it. What I have to say about the path of voice in *Moby-Dick* sometimes parallels Robertson-Lorant in her analysis of the adult Melville's temperament, his martial bearing and periodic viciousness toward his children, servants and wife and probable physical violence toward the latter.[28]

Parker, who states in his Preface that he is no retained attorney, as he finds nothing in Melville that needs defending, passes lightly over these matters. His biography represents a culmination of the Romantic sensibility I'm criticizing here, which still characterizes professional academia in its prostration before an Idea of Genius, its ignorance of life as lived by most human beings on the planet, its cultivated naievete. My approach coincides with Parker's only in what is a minor theme for him, and one which he does not contemplate as I do in light of recent literature about advertising and propaganda: Melville's "ambition," as Parker puts it, "to carry on Gansevoort Melville's role as national propagandist, or even orator of the English-speaking peoples..."[29]

This is where my study diverges from the second school, for I wish to question the ubiquitous premise it uncritically accepts from the first, the premise upon which thousands of pages of Melville studies are founded: namely, that Ishmael is a candid, reliable narrator capable of seeing, comprehending and dispassionately rendering his story and its protagonist, Ahab—or, as Parker puts it, that Ishmael is "biographer of the last voyage of the *Pequod*."[30] I mean to demonstrate instead that if the narrator is a biographer, he is an unreliable one, egregiously so, and, further, that the narrative strategy of mesmerizing readers raises major questions about how clearly Melville could see Ahab, and whether the author was not himself dazzled and mesmerized by his creation.

Pursuing these questions, my first chapter shows how Ishmael's sumptuous language belies what is actually happening—a stiff, frustrated man hates a whale—by presenting it in the charged and heightened terms of tragedy. The second chapter considers narrator and protagonist in light of literature about narcissism, and examines how the narrator loses himself in the protagonist. In the third chapter I discuss the imagery of trance and seduction that permeates the novel. In the fourth I discuss the appetite for vengeful fusion that imparts such power to the narrative voice.

I am fortunate to have found William Cain of Wellesley College, editor of the series in which this work is being published. If the reception accorded it by previous readers is an indication of how it may be received in academic circles, I expect, assuming it is read, that it will prove disorienting. It may be one of the most unsettling and disorienting studies of Melville the reader has encountered, for I am posing fundamental questions which have seldom been asked, and when asked have not become part of the scholarly mainstream. The interesting reasons why they have not become part of the mainstream, while suggesting much about our success in cutting ourselves off from our Erasmian roots, and from quaint Humanist notions regarding the professional responsibility of the scholar to challenge or at least be intellectually robust and supple enough to be willing to challenge orthodoxy, are matters I will not get into here. Suffice it to say here that there exists a vivid if small body of scholarship thoroughly at odds with the tendency noted already in the 1940's by Fiedler and Kazin to displace analysis of Melville's work by veneration, often obsessive, of Melville as Author.

This body of scholarship includes commentary by prominent Melville scholars like Donald Pease and Lawrance Thompson, as well as lesser-known scholars like Richard Blau, J.J. Boies and Marvin Danields. It includes the trenchant commentary of Trinidadian C.L.R. James and the courageous, astute questions Matthieson raises during the height of McCarthyism about charisma and language. It also includes, awkwardly, random insights by some of the writers who venerate Melville, such as Parker's remarkable insight regarding Gansevoort's and subsequently Herman Melville's ambition to be orator of the English-speaking peoples, an insight Parker does not develop.

Parker lets fall other insights that he does not develop. Illuminating more fully than previous biographers the extent to which Allan Melville (father) "cannibalized" his family, Parker is disappointingly terse regarding the possible effects on the impressionable, insecure son by his charismatic, beloved, oracular, cannibalizing father's inveterate, perdurable daydreaming, fabulously vivid to the daydreamer and the substance of the frequent stories he told his children. One would especially like to know Parker's thoughts about how Herman might have been affected by his father's cardinal daydream: his and his progeny's prerogative to move in "the most exalted circles" due to the royal blood flowing in his veins.[31] Nor does Parker, who essentially skips over the thicket of complications that was Melville's relationship with his mother—oracular in her own right—and the voluminous scholarship exploring it, make one suggestion respecting how that other voice in the writer's ear may reverberate in his fiction, to say nothing of how it may shape Melville's fantasy of his reader.

I bring this up not because of the loss to psychoanalytic literature about Melville—Parker is not interested in psychoanalysis—

but because of the loss to textual scholarship in which he is interested. Having decided, with good reason, that we live in "an era when to write a biography is to expose a pathology," Parker, in his determination not to write such a biography, not to be reductive or engage in "slapdash, hubristic Freudianism"[32] has unreasonably decided simply not to notice one of the most pervasive features of Melville's work: the habitual tone of cold, hardened rage just beneath the surface of great "gusto."[33]

*   *   *   *   *

A last note, in a different key.

Whatever else might be said regarding Plato's banning lyric poets from his Republic, one point seems incontestable: this father of Western thought viscerally understood a terrifying paradox. It is that human beings are animals who *inhabit* metaphors, and that metaphors can be sufficiently potent to move citizens and groups of citizens to actions, actions Plato describes as, in the main, life-destroying.

The larger issue I've intended to raise in my work is about this paradox, about metaphor and also about dissimulation as discussed by Bacon in his little essay ("On Dissimulation"). It has to do with the likelihood that in the corporate university, in the Advertising Age culture, whose coin is Virtual, the consequences of not examining with precision, clarity and sobriety the manufacture of metaphor, and its public uses, are more dire by multiple orders of magnitude than in fifth-century Athens.

Notes

Complete bibliographic information may be found in the Selected Bibliography.

1.   James Baird, *Ishmael*, p. 286.

2.   Bette S. Weidman, "*Typee* and *Omoo*," *A Companion*, p. 103, citing T. Walter Herbert's *Marquesan Encounters*, Harvard U.P. (1980) p. 58.

3.   Kingsley Widmer, "Melville and the Myths of Modernism," *A Companion*, p. 670.

4.   John Bryant, Introduction, *A Companion*, p. xviii.

5.   Robert S. Levine, Introduction, *Cambridge Companion*, p. 5

6.   Elizabeth Renker, *Strike*, p. 56, citing Edwin S. Shneidman.

7.   Levine, Introduction, p. 2, and Andrew Delbanco, Afterword, p. 280, *Cambridge Companion.*

8.   Robert Milder, "Melville and the Avenging Dream," *Cambridge Companion*, p. 256.

9.   Bryant, "*Moby-Dick* as Revolution," *Cambridge Companion*, pp. 78-79.

10.   Edward H. Rosenberry, "Melville's Comedy and Tragedy," *A Companion* , p. 605.

11.   Milder, *Cambridge Companion*, p. 259.

12.   Walter Bezanson, "*Moby-Dick*: Document Drama, Dream," *A Companion*, p. 199.

13.   John Wenke, "Ontological Heroics: Melville's Philosophical Art," *A Companion*, p. 586.

14.   Vincent Kinney, "*Clarel*," *A Companion*, p. 377.

15.   Andrew Delbanco, Afterword, *Cambridge Companion*, p. 285.

16.   Bezanson, *A Companion*, p. 198.

17.   Lawrence Buell, "Melville the Poet," *Cambridge Companion*, p. 136, citing Nina Baym's "Melville's Quarrel With Fiction," *PMLA*, 94 (1979) pp. 909-23.

18.   Denis Donoghue, "In the Scene of Being," excerpted in Harold Bloom's *Ahab*, p. 30.

19.   Harold Bloom, Introduction, *Abab*, p. 1.

20.   Edwin S. Shneidman, "Melville's Cognitive Style: The Logic of *Moby-Dick*," *A Companion*, p. 557.

21.   Rosenberry, "Melville's Comedy and Tragedy," *A Companion*, p. 613.

22.   Milton R. Stern, "Melville, Society, and Language," *A Companion*, p. 438.

23.   M. Thomas Inge, "Melville in Popular Culture," *A Companion*, p. 703.

24.   Bezanson, *A Companion*, p. 197.

25.   Inge, *A Companion*, p. 703.

26.   Martin Bickman, "Melville and the Mind," *A Companion*, pp. 520, 529.

27.   Johannes D. Bergmann, *A Companion*, 2p. 51.

28.   Laurie Robertson-Lorant, *Melville*, pp. 48, 294, 504, 512.

29.   Hershel Parker, *Melville*, p. 642.

30.   Parker, *Melville*, p. xvi.

31.   Parker, *Melville*, pp. 62, 9, 59.

32.   Higgins and Parker, "Reading Pierre," *A Companion*, p. 216.

33.   Parker, *Melville*, p. xviii.

THE PUSHER AND THE SUFFERER

An Unsentimental Reading of *Moby-Dick*

Chapter 1

The World As Will

How clearly does Ishmael see Ahab?

More to the point: how clearly is the narrator of *Moby-Dick* able or willing to see the protagonist?

Such a question has not been asked before. This omission, coupled with the circumstance that, in recent years especially, Melville's book is seldom approached in a spirit other than obeisant, has resulted in a scholarly literature remarkably devoid of scepticism.

The absence of scepticism renders certain questions, and orders of questions, invisible. The question as to Ishmael's capacity to tell the truth about Ahab has been invisible; a nonquestion; and it is a contention of this study that invisible questions, like Melville's "invisible spheres," draw from their property of going unseen a heightened potency to captivate—a phenomenon that Ishmael, the captivating, ethereal, appearing and disappearing narrator of *Moby-Dick*, has mastered.[1] As American readers at the start of the twenty-first century, we are in a position to make visible and ask questions about the novel's properties of enchantment, and about whether the vision of the fictive storyteller Ishmael coincides with that of the actual storyteller Melville, which have until now gone unasked. The inquiry is timely and necessary, for not to question enchantment is to admit and even invite to critical discourse a corrosive sentimentality.

Ishmael, the fictive storyteller of *Moby-Dick*, wants what most first-person narrators in nineteenth-century novels want: to entice, induce and persuade readers to see the events of the story, especially its protagonist, Ahab, with his eyes, the way he sees them. Melville portrays Ishmael as a clear-eyed narrator, and Ishmael portrays Ahab as demonic, but also tragic and heroic. Tragic heroism is the gorgeous palette in the colors of which he paints the words and deeds of the protagonist.

Byron, also enamored of "hero-villains," uses a comparable palette. So do Marlowe and Milton. So, at times, do Dante and Shakespeare. What distinguishes Ahab from his brother demon heroes is not that he is marked by special demonic features peculiar to him, since, as a demon hero, Ahab is not peculiar. Indeed, so far as demon heroes go, he is thoroughly true to form. Nor is the excited, insistent doubleness of the narrative vision unique to *Moby-Dick*, the piquant intellectual thrill Ishmael gets from puzzling over how Ahab can be a fiend but also tragic, or the care with which he cherishes his intellectual perplexity. If Melville, the governing sensibility of Ishmael, is excited by Ahab, so is Marlowe excited by Tamburlaine, Shakespeare by Richard, Milton by Lucifer, Dante by the Borgias, Byron by Manfred, Conrad by Kurtz and, for that matter, Dostoevsky by Raskalnikov. The fraternity has women members. At the quick of the stately *Agamemnon* is Aeschylus' anguished excitement as he imagines Clytemnestra, ferocious, sweeping through the palace doors and flaunting her bloody knife at the chorus, at all Argos, at all Greece. Euripides summons not only fear and pity in his audience, but excitement, as he confronts us with the trembling, triumphant child-killer Medea.

These writers are also, however, palpably, unmistakably saddened: modifying their excitement about the demon hero is a countervailing impulse to come into balance in respect to him. In tragedy this impulse is not equivocal. Fraught with tension though it is, it is there, an ambience, a sanity, a capacity to feel horror, face and feel it through and through, signifying the author's willingness to surrender the considerable pleasures of the double vision for the larger, more serious, more daunting aesthetic purpose of showing the demonism for what it is. It, the demonism, and his own excitement about it, make him fearful. Fearful, he trembles. He viscerally, perceptibly shudders.

What makes *Moby-Dick* unusual—unusual, not unique—and makes all the more pertinent the question of whether the narrator sees the protagonist clearly, is an undertone in Ishmael's voice that suggests he is less interested in seeing through the doubleness than in relishing it. This means that Melville does not, perhaps because he prefers not to, shudder.

The terms of the convention of the reliable narrator are not abstruse. Reader presumes that narrator, judicious, sees tale with open eyes, comprehends it, does not significantly distort it. Ishmael, fond of intellectual abstraction, must convince readers to see Ahab with his eyes because his vision of Ahab is the gravitational center of the book. To Ishmael, Ahab's hunt of the White Whale represents a quest for transcendent truth.[2]

Let us look at exactly what Ahab does.

What Ahab does is to decide that a certain white whale he knows is or may be malevolent, that this whale may and probably did bite off his leg deliberately, because it wanted to humiliate him, and that, as a consequence, he has been turned into a Man With A Mission. His Mission is to pay the whale back.

And Ishmael. What does he do?

Ishmael, lonely Ishmael, hides. Where? In talk. About what? About Ahab's whale, and even more, about Ahab.

The Idea of Ahab is to Ishmael what the Idea of the White Whale is to Ahab.[3] As Ahab apprehends in Moby-Dick immortal Evil, and conceives himself its extirpator, so Ishmael, conceiving himself "the tragic dramatist who would depict mortal indomitableness in its fullest sweep," apprehends in Ahab mortal Greatness: and Greatness, willed, mortal Greatness, rendering the great one insusceptible to the "hypos" of depression that plague this narrator from page one, is the narrator's obsession (130).

To be Great, by willing himself into Ahab, is also Ishmael's way out of his own life.[4] To be Great is to leave himself behind and be transported. His hypos are heavy. They weigh him down. They are to him a terrifying feature of existing in a human body. Because Ishmael is terrified of being human, getting transported requires, for him, proximity to what he fancies is superhuman: a condition which, although entailing suffering, entails the preferable variety of suffering that is, in his eyes, by virtue of its Greatness, hypo-free. He needs a hero to love and envy, at least as badly as Ahab, who also longs to be transported, and in his sleep calls out to Moby-Dick to do it—"'Oh Moby-Dick, I clutch thy heart at last!'" (423)—needs revenge. What is the nature of the heroism Ishmael is disposed to find, and finds, in Ahab?

Decidedly not the heroism of classical or Elizabethan tragedy. In tragedy characters become tragic through recognition and transformation, which makes them more civilized, more malleable and capable of deeper feeling, particularly the feeling of remorse.[5] Aristotle would not call Ahab tragic because Ahab, who suffers not because his spirit expands but because it contracts, not because he's growing but because he's static, does not recognize and does not change. To the contrary, he becomes increasingly rigid and intractable, as does the imagery—stiff, stony or sharp—in which the narrator represents him, breathlessly: from the beginning of the novel, when Ishmael first envisions him "made of solid bronze, and shaped in an unalterable mould"—a mould the narrator likens to Cellini's heroic Perseus—to the end, when he recounts Ahab's final words: "*Thus*, I give up"—not life, reports the reporter, reverentially, but—"the spear!" (110, 468). In the interval Ishmael, awed, will extol Ahab as a figure cold, keen and metallic, praise the "mechanical humming of the wheels of his vitality," his "steel skull" and the "magnet" he sets at Starbuck's brain, and compare, admiringly, the "sharp fixed glance from his eyes" to "invisible needles in...unerring binnacle compasses" (142, 147, 183, 192). As a matter of course, Ahab will rarely cross the narrator's path without being metaphorically turned in an instant into a cannonball, pyramid, mortar, railroad train, anvil, mechanical vice, piece of steel, seam of iron, scythe, keel or harpoon.

Ishmael's imagery of hostile hardness, vengeful piercing or icy transfixing is not confined to Ahab, either. As the story progresses, objects and events even remotely associated with Ahab begin to emulate him—principally, and this is my point, the mesmerized narrative sensibility itself. Cato throws himself on his sword, the whale in the painting impales himself on the ship's masts, and the sperm whale's teeth are "spikes" that act "with impaling force" (281). As the *Pequod* leaves port, the sailors turn, in the eyes of the narrator, into Medieval warriors in serious, if incongruous, need of thawing out, "encased in ice, as in polished armor" as they are. The very ship, when he looks at it, turns into a piercing predator (as well as a zoological anomaly), having sprouted, alongside "vast curving icicles," both "long rows of teeth" and "ivory tusks" (95). Daggoo's cry from the mast-head is, to Ishmael's ears, "stiletto-like," the beaks of sea birds are, to his eyes, "insulting poniards," and the keel of the "vindictive," "ivory-tusked *Pequod*," occasionally drops its tusks and turns into "a shark all fins," an invidiously sharp shark that "gores" and "cuts" waves he calls "malicious." For the narrator, all the above happens beneath a gun-sun emitting "bayonet rays" that shoot down "in stacks," like rounds of ammunition (236, 262, 97, 201, 244, 243, 423).

Human faces, too, are at times, for Ishmael, as for Blake, fiery forges. For Ishmael, more often, other persons, places and things resemble weapons or vaguely spiteful machines. Ahab's glance is "a javelin," Steelkilt's an "unflinching poniard" (358, 213). Fedallah has "steel-like lips," while those of Ahab make Ishmael think of a "vice" (187, 400). He, Fedallah and Ahab, regarding the crew less as human sailors than "tiger-yellow creatures," are pleased that the creatures" appear to be made not of flesh and blood but "steel and whalebone." They row not like men, moreover, or even creatures, but "trip-hammers," and, as such, the air around them vibrates not as it does over human beings hard at work, but "like the air over intensely heated plates of iron" (190, 192). Ishmael exempts no one, not even heavenly sky-hawks, which, though heavenly, are not above wishing—the waves share the wish—literally to stick it to Ahab. "Tauntingly", one such hawk, evidently with nothing better to do, swoops down from the stars so that it can gloat over the sinking *Pequod* and peck at Ahab's flag. The hawk goes down beak up, its wing "frozen" by submerged, annoyed Tastego, his head underwater but his hammer still busy, a cartoon event the narrator treats with unwavering solemnity. While Tashtego hammers, Ishmael goes on mixing metaphors, first turning the *Pequod* into Satan drowning, then giving Satan headgear to wear to his watery funeral, then making Satan's winding sheet—why should it have an emotional range wider than anything else's?—so unaccountably livid it rips: the Satan ship sinks "helmeted" in "torn, enraged waves" become a "shroud" (455, 469).

Since, for the narrator, all the Ages of Man are an Age of Iron, his oath of allegiance to Ahab in the chapter "Moby-Dick" possesses a predictably ferric character, that oath which he "welds" to the rest of the crew's, "hammering" and "clinching" it to theirs until, at last, "Ahab's quenchless feud seemed mine" (155). The narrator's notification to readers that he "seemed," through the mediating ecstasy of his shipmates, to fuse with them and with Ahab, and make the communal "feud" his too, is one of the nimblest understatements in three hundred years of American literature.[6] Fusing with partially-real, largely-fantasied others, and thereby dissolving the boundaries of his identity, is what, in fact, Ishmael does. Fusion is his foremost imaginative preoccupation.

Fusion is also the cardinal dynamic by which he relates, insofar as he relates at all, to other characters, themselves already, early in the novel, "welded into oneness," until, for him and for Ahab, they are "one man, not thirty" (454, 455).

His need to fuse, to love blindly, is what makes the narrator sentimentalize Ahab's hate. Ishmael, whose life in the world, whose hopes, heartbreaks, age, real name, whose past, present and future are altogether nebulous, sees Ahab's hatred as heroic because it is definitive and he lacks definition, because he, along with his shipmates, can fall in place around it, because it simplifies. In that hatred he finds, and becomes, a Voice, oracular, weightless, here but not here, a Fedallah who can speak, for in it he, along with Fedallah and the rest of the crew, leaves behind the burden of himself as gladly as Ahab leaves himself when—and this is the only moment of genuine relief for Ahab in the book—he curses, and thrusts his harpoon at Moby-Dick. Wandering lonely in a universe where he has no human ties, Ishmael sees Great Hatred as ennobled purpose because hatred offers a reason to be on earth, and he is afloat in space.

The untethered, passive, floating Ishmael, whose primary relationship is not with other human beings but with words, sees himself, moreover, not as a man but a boy, an eternal boy with an eternally, unforgettably cruel stepmother and no father to protect him from her, a circumstance that makes his need to associate himself with some form of masculinity, however venal, all the more urgent.[7] In this narrator's eyes, uncompromising hatred is reconfigured as tragic virility, which appears to him heroic. Were he as consummately unthinking as he paints his shipmates, his troubles would be, by means of this reconfiguration, over. He could go down with the ship, or not go down, a zombie dazed and cheery as the others, sanguine in the conviction that, torn, covered with scars and zombie though he be, he fought the good fight at Ahab's side, a weird but loyal Panza to Ahab's weird Quixote. But if music be the food of love, Ishmael's averred intellectual scruples are the food of *Moby-Dick*. With the reconfiguration of Ahab's lethal stubbornness to heroism, the narrator's troubles have only just begun, since Ahab's refusal to change, while it awes Ishmael, also sends him deeper into terror, for in the refusal he reads intimations of hell.

From these intimations Ishmael acquires considerable narrative power: from a sense that he was already, during his adventure aboard the *Pequod*, and is still, now, though the adventure is over, in hell, and is telling and retelling his tale from hell.

He is where he has always been, and it is as though no time has passed. Or, more exactly, as though, in this novel, time cannot pass. Moby-Dick, the infernal seducer, is still, in the Postcript, as changeless as Ahab, his infernal suitor. As changeless as the Gorgon's head upon which the narrator liked and evidently still likes to meditate, shivering with fear and excitement. As changeless, finally, as the "palsied universe" itself, with its Dantesque city of Lima, "tearless," "the strangest, saddest city," which "keeps her ruins forever new," her ghastly countenance—a mirror of Ahab's—the "rigid pallor of an apoplexy that fixes its own distortions" (167-8, 170).

Lima's dry whiteness suggests the frozen whiteness of a face, a place, a moment stopped and breathless, the same moment, sentient but petrified, we see in the opening pages of *The Encantadas*. We have entered the inverted she-world—Nature Herself—of the stilled, numbed horrific that haunts Melville's later works, and haunts the often-cited diary entries of the fear and depression he felt when he crawled, infant-like, in the Egyptian pyramids.[8]

The thrill into which the protagonist lifts the narrator, augmented by the narrator's hushed, exalted imagery, makes *Moby-Dick* sound like serious epic, and solicits readers to approach it as such. Readers do, since there is something in us, and Melville knows this, that disposes us to accept the solicitation.

Such a disposition obtains even among sophisticated readers, D.H. Lawrence, for example, who sees in Melville's fascination with the pre-Christian world of the pyramid and the pre-Christian, virtually prehistoric or ahistoric world of *Typee*, vestiges of the Heroic Primitive—Lawrence makes little distinction between the two—he so esteems.[9] Lawrence is charmed, and Lawrence approves *Moby-Dick*'s "hero-villain;" upon discovering that Melville feels most at home with sea creatures, Lawrence does not feel the least queasy. The reason is that he frankly enjoys the misanthropy of the book, and its commotion. That is why he is not troubled, either, by the dead stillness at the heart of the commotion, a waveless, muffling stillness discernible despite the rhetorical strategies used to conceal it, particularly the narrator's strategies of disappearance.

Ishmael, smart, disappears in his tale because invisibility suggests omniscience, and omniscience suggests impartial, disinterested and clear, if double, vision, vision unimpaired by needs, and it is imperative for a work such as *Moby-Dick*, whose narrator readers are meant to trust, that we trust and believe the narrator can see clearly.[10] What in fact transpires is that the narrator disappears behind his readers' eyes.

Disappearing behind readers' eyes means that Ishmael tells us what we see and how we see it. In his presentation of Ahab, the narrator instructs in how to look without seeing.

There is a delay of fifty pages between Ishmael's first mention of Ahab, in "The Ship" chapter, and the occasion of Ahab's first appearance on the *Pequod*'s decks. This delay is one of several, the longest being that which occurs between the narrator's first mention of the White Whale and the first sighting. Delay, orchestrated, creates anticipation, and Ishmael stokes readers' anticipation by speaking of Ahab in a certain manner, a manner hushed and mysterious, before introducing him in the plot. By means of the delay, he narratively reproduces and places readers in a situation exactly parallel to his own when he first signs aboard the *Pequod*.

Ishmael has not yet seen Ahab. He will not see him until the *Pequod* is well out to sea. About the figure of Ahab, however, he begins to create a specific emotional aura, an aura not of the observed, corporeal Ahab but the mythic Ahab he began creating earlier, in his talk with Captain Peleg. The aura is heady, and Peleg, as reported by Ishmael, contributes generously to it. When Ishmael says he wants to see the world, Peleg replies by asking if he has seen Captain Ahab. Peleg proceeds to explain how Ahab lost his leg to Moby-Dick, narrative ensues, and Ishmael returns to the subject of the invisible captain to whom he will soon entrust his life. He seems reassured to learn that Ahab, as he tells readers, belongs to a community of whale-hunting Quakers with Biblical names, "fighting Quakers," he calls them, Quakers "with a vengeance" (71).

Now begins the narrator's first extended portrait of Ahab, whom, dramatically, he does not call by name and says we will not meet "as yet."[11] Readers may remember that in the fictive construct Ishmael is a storyteller, the story he is telling occurred in the past, and he, to say nothing of Melville, is continuously choosing how he wants to tell it. His choice of a first-person plural form of address, his choice narratively to reproduce a sequence of events in which Ahab's shadow precedes and ushers him in, and the figures of speech he chooses to portray Ahab, suggest the particular atmosphere about his story he wishes to evoke, an atmosphere which will affect readers in a particular way. That atmosphere is one of fear and excitement:

> So that there are instances among them of men, who, named with Scripture names—a singularly common fashion on the island—and in childhood naturally imbibing the stately dramatic thee and thou of the Quaker idiom; still, from the audacious, daring, and boundless adventure of their subsequent lives, strangely blend with these unoutgrown peculiarities, a thousand bold dashes of character, not unworthy a Scandinavian sea-king, or a poetical pagan Roman. And when these things unite in a man of greatly superior natural force, with a globular brain and a ponderous heart; who has also by the stillness and seclusion of many long night-watches in the remotest waters, and beneath constellations never seen here at the north, been led to think untraditionally and independently; receiving all nature's sweet or savage impressions fresh from her own virgin voluntary and confiding breast, and thereby chiefly, but with some help from accidental advantages, to learn a bold and nervous lofty language—that man makes one in a whole nation's census—a mighty pageant creature, formed for noble tragedies. Nor will it at all detract from him, dramatically regarded, if either by birth or other circumstances, he have what seems a half-wilful overruling morbidness at the bottom of his nature. For all men tragically great are made so through a certain morbidness. Be sure of this, O young ambition, all mortal greatness is but a disease. But, as yet we have not to do with such an one...(71).

The narrator's eloqence, like the eloquence of any fine orator, sounds like profundity. It would seem a pity to suggest that he is not being profound, but rather amassing fleets of dubious assertions. Such, however, is my suggestion. Ishmael will often repeat, vary and amplify these assertions. Each serves to elevate Ahab to a superhuman stature. How?

Ahab resembles a sea-king and also an ancient Roman. He is superior, intellectually and physically, and has, in addition, a superior heart. He is magnificently independent. He is bold. He would fit well in a pageant; he is enough to be, himself, a country; he is made for tragedy. Not the least of his gifts, incidentally, is oratory.

He is also "morbid." His morbidness even seems willful—but, says Ishmael, without blinking an eye, willful morbidness is endemic to mortal greatness.

In the face of the narrator's sumptuous prose the reader may lose sight of what is literally going on.

Ahab is chasing a whale.

Ahab loathes the whale and wants to kill it.

Ahab's loathing is, to himself and the narrator, a fetish object, and that is why Ishmael cannot let Ahab look directly at himself, see Ahab dispassionately or let him be clearly seen by crew or reader.[12] To let Ahab be seen would be to expose the fetishistic trappings of his loathing, and reveal an Ahab who bears little resemblance either to who he himself says he is, according to the narrator, or to the narrator's account of him. This Ishmael cannot do, for what is left of the protagonist, when we see not with but through the narrator's lovesick eyes, is a figure for whom loathing is not simply a habitual feeling but the only feeling he has, a figure whose sole desire is to outwit, hunt down and kill, a figure to whom literally nothing on earth, except an Enemy—at present a white whale—is real.[13]

This figure's loathing is neither heroic nor tragic, which is not to say that it lacks a simulated form of grandeur. What imparts to Ahab's loathing its seeming grandeur is Ishmael's talk. Grandeur results from the circumstance that Ishmael's manner of talking and the subject he is talking about are emotionally disconnected.

Moby-Dick's power, that is, comes not from what the protagonist is doing but from the narrator's manner of representing what he is doing. Ishmael, afraid of sinking in himself, needs to see what Ahab is doing as occurring on a heroic plane of experience. If Ahab, the hater, is a hero, then Ishmael can at least temporarily forget his hypos—his feelings—by orally partaking, in a sense suckling, from Ahab's hardness, which he does by shaping Ahab in powerful words. By idolizing the rageful dictator, Ishmael is seeking access to that godhead of rage which, circumventing and disdaining the womb, will bring him to life, a life with will but without feeling. Ultimately this narrator's way of talking—and talking is as necessary to him as breathing—assumes a "life" of its own, the simulated life devoted to and empowered by simulated feeling.

Simulated feeling is feeling that is worked up.[14] In *Moby-Dick*, one of the loudest of books, the narrator works up feeling to disguise how averse he is actually to feel, unless one denominates as "feeling" the condition of permanent excitement that the loveless, unloved narrator, whose own rage is locked in his hypos, aspires to in his clandestine symbiosis with his tantrum-addicted captain.[15]

The peculiarly held-in quality of Ishmael's voice, moreover, the sense of his being not in but behind his eyes, the sense of an impending explosion that does not happen, also describe what may have been Herman Melville's characteristic public demeanor in life. It was evident when, for a brief period, he gave public lectures, an occupation for which he seems to have had little enthusiasm, and to which he may have been forced, or, perhaps, simply nudged, relentlessly, by family pressures. Family pressures of many kinds were, as numerous biographers have pointed out, a potent fact of Melville's life from at least the age of twelve, when his father died.[16] After the relative financial failure of *Moby-Dick*, the complete failure of *Pierre*, and the writer's deepening depression, family pressures coalesced into a demand, transmitted steadily from various quarters of both the Gansevoort and Melville households, that Herman, whose 1856 trip to the Holy Land had failed to make him any merrier, shape up. If at the age of thirty-seven he was not to turn out like his father, dependent on in-laws, then it was time he began providing for himself, his wife, his growing family and his widowed mother, now living with him.

These were the circumstances under which Melville embarked on his speaking tours, circumstances he may have felt as a strange reprise of his early adolescence, when, abruptly, the demand came for him to take care of others, including his mother. Perhaps it was a certain resentment at having to give the lectures in the first place, at those who pressured him into it as well as those who came to hear him, a resentment threaded through and complicated, as it had always been, with insecurity and shyness, that exasperated his listeners. Their frustration at the tense, strained, dull manner in which the author spoke, standing motionless on the platform, not looking up from his notes, was remarked by local newspaper men who attended. In his biography of Melville, Edwin Miller cites Merton Sealts, Jr., who examined newspaper accounts of the lectures of 1856. They are often caustic. A "nasty reviewer" in Charleston wrote:

> "Some nervous people...left the hall; some read books and newspapers; some sought refuge in sleep, and some, to their praise be it spoken, seemed determined to use it as an appropriate occasion for self-discipline in the blessed virtue of patience" (*Melville*, 294).

In Auburn, New York, another reporter attacked Melville's

> "inexcusable blundering, [and] sing-song, monotonous deliv-
> ery. It was the most complete case of infanticide we ever heard
> of; he literally strangled his own child." (*Melville*, 294)

The reporter's metaphor is prescient, given the imagery of torture,
murder, asphyxiation and infanticide that fills Melville's fiction.
What the audiences heard, as Melville punished them and himself
by testing how long they would put up with him and let him bore
them to death, was a man privately, as was his custom, choking,
choking with rage.[17]

In Ishmael we see the blocked, oblique attempt to express this
rage. Ishmael cannot feel his own rage without getting close to
Ahab, and the narrator's only means of getting close to Ahab is by
orally sculpting him, by touching and controlling him, and court-
ing his image, in words, for as a character he not only does not
come near his captain; Ahab never even sees him. It's true that
Ahab gives no sign of seeing any of the other sailors either, except
when they get in his way or when he seeks their help to expedite
his pursuit of Moby-Dick. This includes Pip, who, divested of
Ishmael's synedoche, has minimal life as a character, and whose
dialogue with Ahab, like Ahab's dialogue with Starbuck in "The
Symphony," is among the most self-consciously literary in the
novel.[18] The narrator's voice, with all its wit and giddiness, is less
than life-like because Ishmael, forbear of Bartleby, prefers not to
feel his feelings—prefers, simply, not to feel alive. His words rush
in torrents because his mouth is the locus of his feeling alive, the
place where he can to some degree tolerate the feeling, and the
instrument by which he monitors it.

The fictive Ishmael, we remember again, controls the fictive
Ahab. Ahab does not see him because Ishmael, for the purposes of
his story, does not choose that Ahab see him. For Ahab to see
Ishmael might make the latter feel himself. This is what Ishmael is
afraid of, since feeling himself would mean having to feel the emo-
tions locked up in his hypos. Having "nothing particular to interest me on shore," having "a damp, drizzly November in my soul"
is why he goes to sea in the first place. He does not like that
November feeling; it makes him, he hints, want to kill himself or
someone else. He drops the hints casually, playfully, mentioning
that in his daydreams of assaulting passersby, he performs the
assaults without passion or even pleasure. Rather, he envisions
himself a mechanical killer, pouncing "methodically" and "delib-

erately," a killer emotionally disconnected from what he is doing
(12).

The tightly condensed first paragraph of the novel is the only
place the tightly-controlled, self-censoring narrator openly speaks
of his own hostility, and the jocular tone of his voice here as else-
where adroitly draws attention to itself and away from what he is
saying. Facetiousness is one of Ishmael's favorite hiding places. We
may, for example, read "all men tragically great are made so
through a certain morbidness. Be sure of this, O young ambition"
the way we might read "It is the image of the ungraspable phantom of life; and this is the key to it all" (14), as the type of glib
undercutting he often resorts to, especially in the first third of the
book, after seeming to be serious about what he says. Such dex-
terity in undercutting himself is an essential item of Ishmael's narrative skill. By appearing to confide in readers, then warning us to
beware of confidence men, the narrator renders himself supremely
elusive; he also dares readers either to believe or disbelieve his
claims regarding where he has been and who he is.[19]

If Ishmael is modern, however, he is not post-modern. He does
not want to be known or caught himself, but he does want what
he says to be believed. As intent on readers believing though not
knowing him as he is on Ahab not seeing him, he simulates omniscience, hides even his hiding place, and disguises his absence by
dispersing himself in his talk, for talking, particularly talking
about Ahab's brain and Moby-Dick's body, is his preferred means
of disappearing. One might say that Ishmael does not so much disappear then reappear in his story, as disappear then remind us he
is not there and not to be found. Interestingly, the moments when
he most vividly descends into the plot often occur when he loses
consciousness, regaining it only when he senses danger. He falls
asleep and wakes in Queequeg's arms, recounting then the one
memory in his book, of the nightmarish day when he fell asleep as
a child and woke feeling an invisible hand in his. He falls asleep or
almost does during his watch at the *Pequod*'s wheel, and almost
falls asleep standing in the mast-head.

Falling, becoming unconscious, is what the narrator longs to
do and can't. By conceiving Ahab as a figure who will not fall, who
wills himself not to fall, who sleeps, when he sleeps at all, sitting
bolt upright in a chair, and by valorizing Ahab's will to vengeance
as an heroic act, Ishmael numbs himself against his own longing
and shields himself in Ahab's invulnerability, which is actually

impenetrability, as thoroughly as the whale mincer ritually shields himself in the cassock of the whale's genital and appropriates to himself its potency.

The disappearing narrator, in other words, makes Ahab his idol, makes Ahab aggressive, undepressed and monumental because he himself feels down and out, powerless and small. Ishmael endows Ahab with a thundering voice because Ishmael is afraid of stillness, because in stillness lie his feelings and his numbness. That the rage which attracts him to Ahab is not alive but fossilized, that Ahab's emotional iciness, which makes him unable to cry, is remarkably analogous to arid Lima, which so unnerves Ishmael because it seems neither dead nor alive (167-8), analogous to frozen Herculaneum, where skeletons appear to him not dead but "enchanted" in "attitudes," (416) are possibilities the narrator cannot consider.

He cannot because he needs to conceive still, unchanging, furtively decaying Lima as purely feminine—a city transfixed in hypos, like himself—and Ahab as purely masculine. In order not to feel his fear and, at the same time, afraid of feeling nothing, he tells a story full of noise and fury, with a protagonist whose ideal man is fifty feet high, with a brass forehead, no heart, no eyes to see what is in front of him (390), but—lest he be, somehow, overlooked—a tremendous voice, who will exclaim, intending no irony, that feeling, feeling, feeling is enough for mortal men.[20]

This image, Ishmael's fantasy of maleness, derives from Calvin's reading of *Genesis*, the Book that definitively fixes and instates the iconic male and female who rule Ishmael's imagination. It is quite consonant with the portrait of the narrator offered here that he should find contemptible the Jesus figure of the New Testament, vaguely androgynous, inspiring, as he says, those "soft, curled, hermaphroditical Italian pictures in which his idea has been most successfully embodied...destitute as they are of all brawniness," suggesting "nothing of any power, but the mere negative, feminine one of submission and endurance" (315). The Calvinistic Old Testament god upon Whom Ishmael models his Ahab, autochthonously masculine, has a notoriously short fuse, and does not readily submit or endure. While sometimes angry, He never cries, and neither does Ahab, though, as reported by the narrator, he tells Starbuck, the day before the final chase, "I seem to weep" (444).

Precisely what this means, precisely what one is doing when one says about oneself, "I seem to weep," is less than clear, but the expression beautifully illustrates Ahab's extravagant attentiveness to himself, his theatricality, and the sense that he is at all times, simultaneously, on stage and in his own first row, performing to himself. He would like to relent but can't, the narrator implies.[21] The character's actions and words, however, as reported by Ishmael, demonstrate just the opposite, as he repeatedly chooses, rather than to face potentially transformative truths, such as his aging and the loss of his leg, to turn away from them, as he operatically turns his face away from Starbuck at the end, blanching the mate's face "to a corpse's hue with despair" (445). More importantly, in each instance Ishmael aggrandises Ahab's avoidance.

And that, finally, is what cries out, despite Ishmael, from Ishmael's story: how Ahab's malice serves, with startling efficiency, a self-alienating function for himself, narrator and crew, putting each, like a stranger, beside himself. For it is startling how little Ishmael permits Ahab actually to see into himself. Instead of genuine insight, he gives Ahab a lofty tongue. Instead of having a headache, Ishmael's Ahab decides he's wearing—forced to wear—the Iron Crown of Lombardy. Preoccupation with having to wear the Iron Crown of Lombardy enables Ahab to rise above his headache, and enables Ishmael to rise with him. Having to contend with a headache or the loss of a leg might make a character feel who he is by feeling his body, but the scale of excitement the narrator requires quite precludes him, Ahab or readers from feeling who they are.[22] The antithesis of tragic action, which is poignant precisely because the tragic hero becomes more human and uncertain, more a feeling organism, so that the audience can see itself in him, Ishmael's narrative intention would appear to be, by elevating and enlarging Ahab, to abase and diminish readers.

A narrator who abases, or debases, readers, puts them into a very particular relation to his book. We may wonder where we are being led, and to what end, for in each scene that suggests a possible relenting by Ahab, or exposure of his stubbornness as stubbornness, Ishmael wraps the stubbornness in heroic talk. This includes such chapters as "The Candles," when, although Ahab initially speaks of blindness with fear, his talk promptly reverts to a threat to harpoon any sailor who disobeys his orders, and Ishmael's to a simile likening Ahab to a "lone gigantic elm" (418).

In "The Symphony," as he prepares to send his sailors to their almost certain doom, Ahab will cry one tear, but that is enough to send the narrator, along with Starbuck, reeling. Instead of wondering at the paucity of Ahab's grief, he will laud the single tear as an object of veneration: "nor did all the Pacific contain such wealth as that one wee drop" (443).

In these and other instances when Ahab will proclaim that he cannot help himself, that he serves cosmic Forces, that he is Their agent, readers, parting company from the narrator, can entertain an alternative interpretation: that Ahab's remaining in the same state of misery at the end of the novel as he was at the beginning, a misery with no notable modulations, makes him not a heroic or even pitiable figure, but rather one who, in a fundamental sense, does not feel, not his misery and little else.

Again, the exceptions seem to prove the rule. Richard Chase remarks that the image of the setting sun is one of the most moving in all of Melville's fiction, and the "Sunset" chapter in *Moby-Dick*, where Ahab sits alone gazing out to sea, is one of several passages that might illustrate the "humanities" of Ahab upon which Peleg boisterously insists. Here too, however, rather than give Ahab a chance for introspection, the narrator endows him with hyperbolic tropes and images of hardness. Ishmael's voice is not contemplative but tense with excitement. His excitement suggests that Ahab's pronouncement to the gods that his soul is grooved to iron rails is not only not a source of sorrow to him or the narrator, but the salient proof of how special he is.

> Swerve me? ye cannot swerve me, else ye swerve yourselves!
> Man has ye there. Swerve me? The path to my fixed purpose
> is laid with iron rails, whereon my soul is grooved to run.
> Over unsounded gorges, through the rifled hearts of moun-
> tains, under torrents' beds beds, unerringly I rush! Naught's
> an obstacle, naught's an angle to the iron way! (147)

The novel's power, its "iron way," is the elation in the narrator's voice when he imagines Ahab imagining himself as hardness—here, a locomotive—personified, and he imagines this incessantly. Ishmael, scared to be alive, depressed at the prospect, is excited by Ahab and needs to excite readers too. Ishmael would rather be excited than depressed, and makes of Ahab a figure whose force of personality, especially through his way of talking, can lift Ishmael out of himself. It is Ishmael, in transports, being lifted, Ishmael longing to be and being electrified by the Ahab he fantasizes muttering defiantly at sunset to the bullying gods, just as Ahab wants to be electrified in "The Candles," whose voice rings out in the preceding passage.

We may be disinclined, however, to hear what is being said. The preference to not hear but, instead, to be swept away, is why *Moby-Dick* is typically read as an object lesson, and Ahab's arrogance as Melville's foreshadowing gesture that he is headed for a tragic fall.[23] Such readings reassure us that we are in strong hands, that Melville knows what he is doing.[24] They also exhibit deafness to the narrative tone of voice, which is not one of tragic innuendo, but exhilaration. An ominous note is present, to be sure, as there is ominousness in Ishmael's periodic reminders that Ahab is demented, but the narrator's treatment of Ahab lacks not only the sobriety that invests tragic action. Missing also, since Ishmael does not need and cannot use an Ahab who feels himself, but one who sees himself in powerful images, is a single moment of authentic self-appraisal.

The absence of such a moment suggests that the bearing of the narrator towards his hero resembles that of a fanatic.

A closet fanatic. For Ishmael to convince himself that his fantasized symbiosis with Ahab is equivalent to life, he must convince himself that Ahab's hate represents a special, higher form of rectitude. He does—it is not too difficult for him—and, convinced, exults.

In his exultation he appears not to care that Ahab's superhuman stature, and the rhetorical effort needed to maintain it, causes the fictive protagonist literally to petrify in his, the fictive author's, hands. Nor does the narrator care, or even notice, that he begins paying tribute to a statue, since the statue's immobility, which he perceives as heroic, far from giving him grief, is for him evidence of superhumanness. In the Hotel de Cluny passage, where a statue represents manliness defeated and castrated, the narrator's voice, imagining himself as Ahab imagining himself as the sculpture, is that of exultation. Creating an Ahab who does not dare feel what he is doing, Ishmael aggrandises Ahab's coldness by using every metaphoric, allusive, symbolic resource in his impressive store to persuade readers that human emotion is an inconvenience Ahab has risen above. Thus considered, it is the protagonist's willed refusal to feel and the narrator's willed aggrandisement that ravage Ahab, not a struggle with the cosmic meanings of the White

Whale, and it is Ishmael's own fear of feeling that stiffens within
and at last petrifies his hero.[25]

Having opened this chapter by asking how clearly the narrator of *Moby-Dick* sees the protagonist, and proposing that the
answer is none too clearly, I will conclude by asking a related question, drawn from the often-cited letter that Melville, on complet-
ing *Moby-Dick*, wrote to Hawthorne. What does it mean for an
author to declare, "I have written a wicked book, and feel spotless
as the lamb"?[26]

To this reader it means that *Moby-Dick* enacts between writer
and reader the inverse of the cathartic dynamic. That is to say, the
novel intends to arouse regressive desires, and thereby bring audience and narrator into a collusion the cohering principle of which
is hate.[27]

The present study aims to interpret problematic features of
Melville's greatest novel, in particular its ambience of diffuse, subtle enmity. It seems to me that even if one knows nothing whatever of Herman Melville's life, his fiction alone gives the impression
that he was habitually in a state of anger which habitually explod-
ed because he habitually denied it. Furthermore it seems plausible
to suggest, informed by recent biographies, that the way Melville
lived publicly with his denied anger, a way he learned as a child
and never forsook, was to bury it, to become depressed and yearn
for strong male figures.[28]

The "buried" quality of Melville's sensibility, especially in the
years following the publication of *Mardi*, and a sense that the
writer was continually, vainly struggling against a terror of being
closed in—caught, trapped and kept—by a "thing" that might or
might not be human, is one of the richest mysteries of his work. It
is also his signature nightmare, ever-metamorphosing, from the
recurring mummy imagery in *Moby-Dick* and *Pierre*, to the claus-
trophobia he describes in his travelling diary, to the verbal density
of *Pierre* and *The Confidence Man*, which, for some readers,
buries character, plot, and, finally, reader.[29] The vision of Melville
as a man buried within himself became a virtual tradition with
early biographers, from Parrington, who depicts him as having
buried himself in the tomb of the Customs House, to Edwin Miller,
who sees the novelist, like the narrators of "I And My Chimney"
and "The Piazza" as an achingly lonely figure, buried alive under
domesticity and neglect by the reading public.

Images of being buried alive, of suffocation, strangulation, or being confined in a cramped place with not enough air to breathe, are not unique to Melville. As Charles Feidelson shows, fears of asphyxiation appear in the work of other major nineteenth-century American writers, including Hawthorne, Poe and Dickinson. Perhaps Melville in his early life seeming to be driven by a fear of staying still, and Hawthorne, with a different temperament, by a fear of moving, reflect a primitive terror of having one's breath, the breath with which one speaks and writes, stolen by strangers. ·

This would support Lawrence's remarks concerning the totemic aspects of both writers' works. It may also shed light on the extraordinary image of antique Adam, prematurely buried and subsisting in a trance state in which he does not breathe or move but is not dead. Breathlessness, the burial of feelings, and the erosion of clear distinctions between the states of life and death, may also play a part in Lawrance Thompson's impatient response to *Moby-Dick*.[30] Thompson may be reacting less to Melville's overt anger at a god he conceives as dictatorial, calculating, and, at the same time, mysteriously preconscious, than to the novelist's covert replication of this god in relation to readers.

Coming chapters will propose that Melville fears and hates his readers, whom he imagines as powerful, opaque, possibly impenetrable and immensely wicked. Because he sees the reader in this manner, as a "thing" which may also be a person, his need to control our responses, and to punish, is intense and unremitting. The god whom Melville thus replicates in his relation to readers resembles the New Old Testament god whose lineaments began to be drawn in the Reformation, and redrawn by Jonathan Edwards: a not quite extinct volcanic figure who plays with, teases and frightens rather than erupts, and who, burying his rage and sitting atop it, oversees but does not feel.

It may be just this act of overseeing, this frighteningly accurate, if unintended, presentation of how a psyche blocked in its natural impulse to unfold an authentic emotional life learns to oversee its feelings rather than feel them, that accounts for the adulation *Moby-Dick* receives in the academy.

Notes

1.   Ishmael's dissolution into his voice is frequently noted. As Sharon Cameron puts it, the narrator "does become pure voice, relin-

quishing his life as a character" (*The Corporeal Self*, p. 66). In his considerably original *The Body Impolitic*, especially pp. 59, 83, 90, Richard Blau speaks of the narrator's excited, "uneven breath" as he loses himself in Ahab, who, "Identifying ...his will with the whole of the self...is Ishmael's false self."

2.   The idea that *Moby-Dick* represents a heroic search for truth pervades both Melville's vision of his novel, as Renker points out in her Introduction (*Strike*, p. xvi), and recent criticism, as can be seen in many essays in the *Companions* and in A. Robert Lee's 1985 anthology, *Reassessments*, where it is axiomatic. As Lee puts it, Melville invites us "to explore the Protean ways in which Truth undergoes definition," p. 74. In "Melville's Quarrel with Fiction," (*PMLA* 94, pp. 909-923), Nina Baym says "the quest for truth" is the presumptive basis of his novel, adding,

> The notion of truth and language are wrought into the texture and form of *Moby-Dick* to such an extent that to criticize these ideas would be to put into question the ground from which the work had been constructed.

The ground from which *Moby-Dick* is constructed is precisely what I am questioning.

3.   Hegel's speculations regarding the transcendental dimension of history, especially history's "heroes," and Schopenhauer's architectonics in *The World as Will and The World as Idea* influenced German and English Romanticism, American Transcendentalists and Melville. Schopenhauer's "Will," Hegel's "Absolute freedom and terror," Kant, Goethe and Rousseau—along with de Sade—gave Neitzche the stuff that dreams are made of as he made his *ubermenschen*, who bear material resemblances to Ahab and to Emerson's Representative Men. William H. Shurr discusses the possible importance to Melville of Schopenhauer's chapter, "Metaphysics of the Love of the Sexes" ("Melville's Poems," *A Companion*, p. 363). John Wenke looks at Melville's interest in German as well as pre-Socratic metaphysics ("Ontological Heroics," *A Companion*, pp. 568-570).

4.   The driven, suffering persona that wills but does not feel appears frequently in studies of narcissism, and in Neal Tolchin's *Mourning, Gender and Creativity in the Art of Herman Melville*, Charles J. Haberstroh Jr.'s *Melville and Male Identity*, Robert Martin's *Hero, Captain and Stranger* and Judith Fetterley's *The Resisting Reader*. Psychiatrist Alexander Lowen, a writer who elucidates much theoretical work on what Freud came to call primary and secondary narcissism, suggests that narcissistic personalities are inclined to imagine the world as a recalcitrant body to be mastered, and to imagine their own bodies as the instrument of mastery:

> ...they see the body as an instrument of the mind, subject to their will. It operates only according to their images, without

feeling. Although the body can function efficiently as an instrument, perform like a machine, or impress one as a statue, it then lacks "life." And it is this feeling of aliveness that gives rise to the experience of the self (*Narcissism*, p. 8).

Not feeling alive, Lowen says, creates the sense of being an "imposter."

5.   The "evolutionary theme" and "the prominence given to the evolution of civilization," are conceptual premises of H.D.F. Kitto's *Greek Tragedy,* enunciated specifically on p. 64. Kitto, one of the eminent post-World War One soldier scholars working in the tradition of Croce, conceives the tragic effort as one through which, in the end, the idea of civilization itself is reaffirmed. Robert Fagle's Introduction to his 1966 translation of the *Orestia* addresses the same idea.

6.   When Newton Arvin clutched hold of such Ishmaelian qualifiers, in particular Ishmael's "seemed"'s, as in "Ahab's quenchless feud seemed mine" (*Moby-Dick*, p. 155) and "almost"'s, as in "almost every soul on board desired a lowering" (*Moby-Dick*, p. 200) he launched armadas of scholars on a Mission of their own: to save the narrator from the process of infantilization the novel itself portrays (Arvin's *Herman Melville*, p. 171). With his qualifiers Ishmael implies that, although tempted, he was not really party to the delirium of his shipmates, or if he was, he grew up and out of it. But the narrator's innuendo that with time he has gotten a heart of wisdom is flatly contradicted by his story, for the secretive, rueful Ishmael recounting his adventure aboard the *Pequod* is, still, unnumbered years after the adventure, dazzled as ever by Ahab. Most scholarship begins by assuming that *Moby-Dick*, an account of "Ishmaelian consciousness" (Brodtkorb, pp. 3-4), shows how Ishmael, once awed by Ahab, evolves, separates from and transcends him, which helps the narrator "recover his will to live" (Arvin, p. 171). See Brodtkorb (*Ishmael's White World*), Arvin, (*Herman Melville*), Bezanson ("*Moby-Dick*: Work of Art," in Moby-Dick: *Centennial Essays*, pp. 30-58), Wolf (*Romantic Re-Vision*, p. 98), Rogin (*Subversive Genealogies*, pp. 111, 116), Gustaaf Van Cromphout ("*Moby-Dick*: The Transformation of the Faustian Ethos," p. 249 in *On Melville*, edited by Louis Budd and Edwin Cady). In my reading Ishmael does not evolve. He devolves.

7.   Haberstroh offers a nuanced, compassionate discussion of how Ishmael's despairing search for love replicates Melville's own. Haberstroh sees Ahab and Ishmael as "inescapably twinned," the narrator a Puer, or "lost boy" for whom, as for Ahab, "survival, not extinction, is the curse." His "constant fascination with Ahab," writes Haberstroh, occasions "Ishmael's final loneliness, which comes from more than his being the last survivor of the *Pequod*'s sinking...when at last he seems most conclusively free of Ahab's monomania...Ishmael also seems most desolate. He did not want to lose Ahab...(*Melville and Male Identity*, pp. 92, 101-102). Psychoanalyst Alice Miller centers her work about narcissism in the idea that grandiosity and depression necessitate each other. She likens the

dynamic to a marriage whose partners are named "Grandiose" and "Depressive" (*Drama*, pp. 43, 44-45 and *Good*, pp. 58, 72, 74).

8.   David Leverenz discusses the continual circling-back of Melville's imagery to "our origins in the sphinx and pyramid, those non-phallic, ambiguously maternal, unrelentingly and inhumanly inscrutable creations of the dead" ("Moby-Dick," in *Psychoanalysis and Literary Process*, ed. Frederick Crews, pp. 103-104).

Richard Chase makes a related point:

> Always in Melville's writings the female body—that Tartarus of Maids—revives some primitive fear, some dark ambiguous awe, some sick revulsion, some guilty, stonelike paralysis...In *Redburn* there were two images of the author: Redburn himself, who would survive and mature, and Harry Bolton, the homosexual youth who was doomed. But Harry Bolton lived on in Melville (*Herman Melville*, pp. 294-5).

9.   *Moby-Dick*'s "strong overtones of primitivism"—Olson, following D.H. Lawrence, praises its "antediluvian mood" (*Call Me Ishmael*)—have been among its most admired features (*Twentieth Century Interpretations of* Moby-Dick).

10.   He disappears, that is, to appear as though omniscient and thereby make his tale more credible. To "be absent from the body is sometimes (not to speak it profanely) to be present with the Lord," writes Charles Lamb, whose humor and gentleness Melville admired ("Oxford in the Vacation" from *The Essays of Elia*, p. 12). Ishmael wishes readers to suppose that if we will only absent ourselves from ourselves, like he does, we will be with the Lord, as he is. Charles Feidelson and Michael Davitt Bell discuss credibility as a fraught issue around which nineteenth-century American novelists tiptoed nervously. In *Novels, Readers and Reviewers*, Nina Baym addresses the difference between credibility and truth. Milton R. Stern contends, and so do other readers who see Melville as postmodern, that Melville is a disillusioned Idealist, for whom there is no truth ("Melville, Society and Language," pp. 433-479, *A Companion*).

11.   Robert Zoellner, troubled by Ishmael, hypothesizes a "pre-literary Ahab" (*The Salt-Sea Mastadon*, p. 94). Bezanson isn't troubled by Ishmael at all, and recommends that readers who are become more "...practiced in Ishmael's range of sensibilities," which Bezanson, along with Ishmael, regards as vast *(A Companion*, p. 186). For him, whatever troubles Ishmael has result from his being a "wild man" with "high metabolism," like the Biblical figure after whom he names himself. Bezanson seems amused that Ishmael names himself "Ishmael;" he finds the chapter "Loomings" "Beethoven-like," and reads it, far from portraying a narrator who's depressed, as demonstrating instead "...the marvellous energies of a racounteur in top form, a first encounter, perhaps, with

Ishmael's hyena laugh, just part of the "'general joke'" (Bezanson, *Moby-Dick*: Document, Drama, Dream," *A Companion*, p. 186).

For Robertson-Lorant and the body of scholarship addressing the Ishmael's skill at making myth, Ahab frequently appears as a perverse Parsifal figure whose Grail is The Whale.

12.   Raisa Nemikin, a terrific student, put it succinctly: "Ahab hates; therefore he is." And if he hates, he must hate like no one has hated before: he must hate Absolutely. Blau, concurring with Quentin Anderson in *The Imperial Self*, says "the central characteristic of Emersonianism" is the "desire for absolute uniqueness. The "true despot," for Blau, "the 'nameless, inscrutable, cozening thing'" that stuns Ishmael" is Ahab's Ego" (*The Body Impolitic*, pp. 87, 100).

13.   The determination to salvage Ahab's putative greatness can be fantastic in its illogic. Although Tyrus Hillway—he is not the only one—calls Ahab "the supreme statement of Melville's 'Everlasting No,'" he finds the 'No,' presumably because it is Everlasting, "heroic in proportions" (Hillway's *Herman Melville*, chp. 6, "The Everlasting No," pp. 78-112, esp. p. 94). Thomas Woodson is not alone in mixing and matching: "Ahab's Greatness: Prometheus as Narcissus, *Journal of English Literary History*, 33 (September, 1966), pp. 351-369. For some readers Ahab is a Knight "defending against chaos" (Rogin, p. 116); for others he is nothing less than "the fate of human dignity" (Walter Herbert's Moby-Dick *and Calvinism*, p. 127), a fate appointed to teach humanity to stop cringing before God (Thornton Booth's "*Moby-Dick*: Standing up to God," pp. 87-93 in *Critics on Melville: Readings in Literary Criticism*, edited by Thomas Rountree). At times, incredibly, Ahab is the Savior Himself: "Ahab, one might say, has taken upon himself the suffering of mankind" (William Braswell's *Melville's Religious Thought*, p. 66). Rowland A. Sherrill says that Braswell's 1943 book, published without benefit of the later research of Leyda and Sealts, nonetheless "...remains an interesting argument about Melville's movement toward scepticism" (Sherrill, "Melville and Religion," *A Companion*, p. 494). The "scepticism" to which Braswell and Sherrill refer has to do the usual reading of Melville as a writer ahead of his time, who "...challenges the contemporary religious community for falling short of the ideals implicit in its own mythic self-conception" (Sherrill, p.494).

14.   Zoellner is describing simulated feeling when he distinguishes "fire-vitality" from "life-vitality" (*The Salt-Sea Mastadon*, p. 204).

15.

> Perhaps you are wondering: Can any human being act total-
> ly without feeling? Does the denial of feeling mean the denial
> of all feeling? In narcissistic individuals, expressions of feeling
> usually take two forms: an irrational rage and a maudlin sen-
> timentality. To act without feeling is to be a monster, but true
> monsters, like Frankenstein's, exist only in our imagination.
> Human monsters are characterized by their irrational rage,
> their sentimentality, and their insensitivity to others
> (*Narcissism*, p. 62).

16.   Edwin Haviland Miller paints a vivid picture of the Melville
household, especially in the days when the father was dying (Miller's
Melville, p. 69). Arvin describes the atmosphere of the home in which
Maria Gansevoort and her eight children were left by the death of her husband as a "demoralizing half-world" (Arvin's *Herman Melville* pp. 24-
28). The sense of being trapped in a "half-world" or Limbo—Howard's
"atmosphere of anxiety" (Leon Howard's *Herman Melville*, p. 18)—may
have helped to foster what William Gilman calls Melville's "addiction to
melancholy" (*Melville's Early Life and* Redburn, p. 233). Tolchin calls it
"chronic grief," and suggests that it stemmed from how deeply Melville
"internalized...Maria's bereavement" and mirrored her depressions
(*Mourning*, pp. 33, 161). According to Renker and others writing of
Melville's domestic life, the private man, often depressed, was also violently explosive toward his wife and family. Walter Kring seems to have
been the first scholar to unearth the now famous 1867 letter from Samuel
Shaw, Melville's brother-in-law, proposing that the family stage a kidnap-
ping to rescue Elizabeth from Melville's sporadic violence. (*New York
Times*, January 24, 1999 Section 1, p. 41)

17.   Scholars disagree about the success of Melville's 1857-1860
speaking tours. James Barbour, citing the earlier work of Merton Sealts,
plus later scholarship, writes that of "existing newspaper reports, the
majority...were favorable" ("Melville Biography", *A Companion*, p. 26).
Howard examines unfavorable newspaper accounts of the Chicago tour
(p. 261), and looks at the role Maria Gansevoort Melville appears to have
played in this and Melville's other careers. Weaver, Arvin, Tolchin and
Robertson-Lorant discuss the intense ambivalence that seems to have
characterized the relationship between the mother and her second, unfa-
vored son, Herman. Weaver's conjectures from Gansevoort family tales
are what sparked the interest of many of the later biographers, and,
though sometimes questioned today, are more often than not supported by
archival research:

> Between Maria and her son there existed a striking personal
> resemblance. From his mother...Melville seems to have inher-
> ited a constitution of very remarkable vigor, and all the white
> intensity of the Gansevoort aptitude for anger (*Herman
> Melville: Mariner and Mystic*, pp. 61-62).

Maria Melville, writes Tolchin, "must have been baffled by this mirror
image of herself—fascinated, and at the same time contemptuously revolt-
ed" (*Mourning*, p. 168). Tolchin's suggestions regarding the manifold
ways Melville's mother alternately undermined her writer son and
"stroked his ego," have been helpful to the present study. So have Arvin's
suggestions about a "perilous intensity of feeling" between mother and
son, and the "depth of injury" to the latter, manifest in Melville's private
life in a "tiger-pit of irritable and contradictory emotionality" (Arvin's
Herman Melville, p. 30).

18.   Although the narrator's own sentimentality regarding Starbuck
and Pip has not often been addressed, Ahab's has. See Marvin E.
Mengeling's "*Moby-Dick*: The Fundamental Principles," in *Emerson
Society Quarterly*, 38 (1st. Qt., 1965), pp. 74-87. Melanie Klein's suggestion in *Our Adult World* regarding the endless need of the narcissistic personality "to make reparation" sheds light on both the melodrama and the
humor in *Moby-Dick*.

19.   Work on the subject of Melville's narrators includes David S.
Reynolds's essay, "'Its wood could only be American!'": *Moby-Dick* and
Antebellum Popular Culture,' in *Critical Essays on Herman Melville's
Moby-Dick*, edited by Brian Higgins and Herschel Parker, pp. 523-544,
Wai-Chee Dimock's *Empire For Liberty* and Edgar Dryden's *Melville's
Thematics of Form*. Especially pertinent to the present study are Dryden's
remarks in Chapter V concerning the imposter-narrator of *The
Confidence-Man*.

20.

> Every narcissistic individual I have encountered "feels" spe-
> cial. I put the word "feel" in quotes because specialness is not
> a body sensation but a mental construct. It is, therefore, a
> matter of belief or thinking rather than feeling. Nevertheless,
> the person who "feels" superior does translate this onto the
> body level, through the ego's dissociating from the body and
> sensing itself above the body (*Narcissism*, p. 106).

21.   Psychoanalyst Marvin Danields discusses "the depression upon
the brink of which he [Ahab] is always standing...He cannot help himself
and will let no one else help him..." Danields describes Ahab as a "con-
firmed hater," and analyzes the pusher-sufferer nexus this way: "...the
paranoid sacrifices love for the sake of power, while the masochist sacrifices power for the sake of love...The paranoid is megalomaniac. He

appears to be as God..." and onto him, writes Daniels, "...the masochist projects his wish for power..." Neither can achieve union through love, so they crave and try to get it through revenge:

> ...vindictiveness functions to effect a reunion with the disappointing beloved one through mutual suffering or, finally, mutual annihilation...The vengeance itself is a form of loving worship.

Daniels cites an essay by Karen Horney about revenge in which she posits an "Ahab personality," which she characterizes as "arrogant-vindictive" ("Pathological Vindictiveness and the Vindictive Character,"in *Psychoanalytic Review*, Vol. 56, #2, 1969, pp. 170, 177,178, 188, 193).

22.   Ernest Becker writes in *The Denial Of Death* that not feeling oneself enables one to imagine oneself immortal. In Mengeling's reading, Ahab is not immortal but, "in fact, dead; though he galvanizes himself into a semblance of life, and stands upon the deck afflicting the crew with the dark and manifold reflection of his disease" ("The Fundamental Principles" in *Emerson Society Quarterly* 38, 1965, p. 78). Daniels and Horney, examining what transpires between the crew and Ahab, discuss the "veneer of civility" and "naive egocentricity" with which "the Ahab personality...humiliates, exploits, frustrates..." ("Vindictiveness," p. 177).

23.   For readers seeking heroes, *Moby-Dick* offers a thousand faces. Bezanson's seminal 1953 paper, "*Moby-Dick*: Work of Art," in Moby-Dick: *Centennial Essays*, pp. 30-58, portrays Ahab as an object-lesson for Ishmael, and, by extension, for readers. Henry Nash Smith, in his paper in the same book, "The Image of Society in *Moby-Dick*," pp. 59-75, has a similar point of view. The two essays together delineate principal lines of criticism of the past fifty years: "This view makes Ishmael" who, in the view of Nash, Bezanson, Arvin, Zoellner, Robinson-Lorant, Parker et al, is "healed" by the end of the book, "rather than Ahab the 'hero'..." (Bezanson, p. 40).

Rogin too considers Ishmael "healed" at the end. The healer is none other than Ahab, who "rescues" the narrator "from his pantheistic fate" (*Subversive Genealogies*, p. 111). William Dillingham concurs. Although noting how the narrator mimics Ahab—"...the Ishmael who has lived through the destruction of the *Pequod* to tell about it sounds remarkably like Ahab on many occasions..."—Dillingham ultimately sees Ishmael as the figure upon whom "Melville builds his theory of survivorship" (*Melville's Later Novels*, p. 142). For an astute but still Ishmael-enchanted reading of *Moby-Dick*, see Dillingham's citation of Sanford E. Marovitz's essay "Old Man Ahab" in *Artful Thunder: Versions of the Romantic Tradition in American Literature*, ed. Robert J. Demott and Sanford E. Marovitz, Kent: Kent State University Press, 1975.

24.   In 1948 Leslie Fiedler suggested that criticism of Melville was becoming overly-enthusiastic appreciation rather than analysis (*Partisan Review*, June 15, 1948). Alfred Kazin agreed and the next year wrote

"Ishmael in His Academic Heaven" (*The New Yorker*, February 12, 1949), in which he deplores the tendency of "to build up a Melville...who was never disorderly except on purpose..." Several decades later the building up was complete. Alan Friedman's *The Turn of the Novel* is representative both in its unquestioning presumption that Ishmael is trustworthy and its cavalier dismissal of earlier readers' "naive" unease. Nonetheless, what Friedman calls Melville's "fine moral openness" (*Turn*, p. 23) is seen by J.J. Boies ("The Whale Without Epilogue" in *Modern Language Quarterly*, Vol. XXIV, #2) and Kingsley Widmer (*The Ways of Nihilism: A Study of Herman Melville's Short Novels*) as nihilism. Boies, remarking that "All of his major protagonists are suicidal, from Tommo to Billy Budd," divides the protagonists between "the obvious suicides" and the "passive" ones who die "by denying the will to live..." ("The Whale Without Epilogue," pp. 174, 175, 176). Sarah Lawall, commenting on Maurice Blanchot's concept of "negative consciousness," makes a similar point (*Critics of Consciousness*, p. 247, citing *Le Livre a venir*, Blanchot).

25.   Lowen notes the bodily rigidity that often characterizes narcissistic personalities, which leads them to adopt a habit of posing in a statuesque manner and "extend[ing] this image to include the idea of nobility" and deification:

> "I can do anything" (omnipotence)..."I am visible everywhere" (omnipresence)..."I know everything" (omniscience). "I am to be worshipped." These, of course, are the attributes of a god. On some deep level, narcissists, and especially psychopathic personalities, see themselves as little gods. Too often, unfortunately, their followers look up to them in that light, too (*Narcissism*, pp. 54, 57, 107).

26.   Letter to Hawthorne of November 17, 1851. *Moby-Dick*, p. 566.

27.   The atavistic pull of *Moby-Dick* was not lost upon some of the novel's first readers, nor upon Nina Baym, Jane Tomkins or Hugh Hetherington, who study the early reviews. Ludwig Lewisohn, writing in 1932 with a straightforwardness and color that does not characterize professional discussion today, sensed the imposture of Melville's narrators: "The final image that arises from all of Melville's work is that of a big bearded violently excited man trying to shout down the whimpering, lonely child in his soul" (*Moby-Dick*, p. 634, from "Melville: Not Even A Minor Master")

28.   D.W. Winnicott's discussion of the "as if" personality offers fresh ways of understanding the nature of the rage in *Moby-Dick*. Lowen cites Freud's statement that "...in narcissism libido is withdrawn from objects in the world and directed onto the ego," so that the narcissist person's only source of pleasure is his inflated self-image:

Narcissism splits the reality of an individual into accepted
and rejected aspects, the latter then being projected upon others. The attack upon these others stems partly from the desire
to destroy this rejected aspect (*Narcissism*, pp. 33, 51).

29.   John Updike, "Reflections: Melville's Withdrawal," *The New
Yorker*, May 10, 1982, pp. 120-147.
   30.

I admire Lawrance Thompson's work on Melville, and the
intensely felt quality of his reading. Like Lewisohn, he reads
with his whole being. Nonetheless, although he senses in
Moby-Dick something devious that bothers him no end, the
original aspects of his study get entangled with his oversim-
plifying conjectures about Melville's childhood and his expli-
cation of the book's infernal theology. He and other scholars
of his generation, such as Edinger and Murray, write at length
about Melville's rebellion against religious and literary con-
ventions of his day, and read passages like Ahab's "Ego non
baptismo te in nomine patris, sed in nomine diaboli!" (*Moby-
Dick*, p. 404) as proof, and certainly the writer was revolting
against convention, as nearly every letter to Hawthorne testi-
fies. But Melville's anger neither began nor ended with con-
ventions or God, Whom, as Ahab says in a interesting image,
he has no long gun to reach (*Melville's Quarrel*, p. 51).

Chapter 2

Narcissism

How does the overt narcissism of Ahab serve, and how is it served by, the veiled narcissism of Ishmael?

How, that is, does the voice of the fanatic resemble that of the advertiser?

And how does the fanatic succeed in making his audience overlook or simply not care that he is a fanatic, and come in time actually to enjoy, frankly or otherwise, his fanaticism?

Readers moved or awed by Ahab, or who agree with the character Stubb that being kicked by an Ahab is a privilege, may find such questions odd. Readers who concur with Ishmael that Ahab is heroic, or who, with the narrator, commiserate with Ahab that Fate, in league with Moby-Dick, has treated him unfairly, so his vengefulness is not his fault—it's Fate's fault—may find literary-critical terms such as "imperial self," with its evocations of grandeur, more palatable than "narcissist." The latter term is used here not as judgment, however, but description, as Freud intended it, and what may be gained by considering the figure of Ahab not as imperial self but narcissistic fanatic is not simply iconoclastic pleasure on my part of exposing Melville's hero. More important is how such a consideration may change the way we read *Moby-Dick*, and change our understanding of what kind of book the fictive and, of course, the actual author write.[1]

What kind of book Ishmael-Melville write is one question. Whether they are indeed writing the same book is another, and brings to mind the phenomena known in mass marketing as "packaging" and in politics as "spin."

29

"Spin" and "packaging" describe ways language is used not to clarify but to befog. They are techniques of selling ideas, and were, as such, objects of scorn to Socrates in his castigation of the Sophists. The accelerating dissemination of ideas as well as goods in the nineteenth century, the concomitant increase of advertising, and its increasing sophistication, helped make "spin" and "packaging" ubiquitous features of twentieth-century culture, an event foreseen by Orwell and by Joyce, who employs Leopold Bloom as a salesman of newspaper advertisements. The preeminent expertise of American advertising agencies both in creating "consumer" "appetite," and in stoking and inciting the "appetite" into the act of purchase, has been internationally acknowledged for fifty years. It was appreciated by Josef Goebbels, Hitler's propoganda minister, who made a project of studying, then using, methods pioneered by American publicists to sell to the German people their Fuhrer's vision of a Thousand Year Reich. The concern expressed in recent years by writers disparate as Adrienne Rich, William Bennett, Paul Fussell, Stanley Fish, Allan Bloom, Norman Podhoretz, Noam Chomsky and Robert Hughes about the degradation of public language into "spin" proceeds from their sense that it now appears to be nationally understood, and hardly a source of outrage, as though it has attained the status of a fact of life, that in advertising, as in propaganda, as in mainstream media, what is requisite is not accuracy, but sounding true.

The imperative to sound true, as distinct from telling or trying to tell the truth, also characterizes what Freud calls "primary" and "secondary" narcissism. To sound, or seem, true—to "spin"—is to persuade others that what I am is not what they observe me do, but what I say I am. To sound true is also to imply that if others believe what I say, rather than believe their own eyes, they will not be sorry.

For the narcissistic personality, dissuading others from believing their own eyes is a life-or-death enterprise, since only by dissuading them can he persuade himself—almost—that he is not lying. Sounding true enables him to picture himself, secretly, as sublime, an image which, for the narcissist, supplants a sense of self. By sounding true, thereby persuading readers to subscribe to his version of the story he tells about Ahab's loathing of the White Whale, the narrator of *Moby-Dick* displaces his hypos of depression by an image of himself as potent and sublime.

How?

For Freud and many practicing psychologists who write on the subject, narcissism has fundamentally to do with the ways a person instates his image of himself as ruler over his feeling of himself. Not daring to feel his feelings, he learns to wield them instead, enacting then observing them from a distance, as in theater. Not daring to feel alive, but needing to, so as not to feel cold and numb, he requires the drama that he is watching, which is lifeless, to seem grander than human life. Because rageful Ahab and melancholic Ishmael need to see themselves as sublime in order to feel alive, they pursue sublimity, pursue it desperately, relentlessly, literally to the ends of the earth, put on and wear, as it were, visions of themselves in front of themselves, and rise above their feelings.[2]

Rising above their feelings is how protagonist and narrator train themselves not to see, feel or know what they are doing, and how they successfully induct in their audiences a corresponding incapacity.

Put bluntly, I am suggesting that the source of *Moby-Dick*'s power is its appeal to atavism and to a fantasized reversion to barbarity. The very opposite of the tragic aesthetic, this brings to mind Eliot's remark about Baudelaire, that he might have thought evil less beautiful had he honestly felt what it is. And I propose further that insofar as Ahab's pursuit of the whale is horrific, the horror, like the narrator Ishmael, is eminently modern, in that it is reported as though the reporter himself is numb, and in that his reporting has the effect, after initially stunning with excitement, of numbing and emotionally immobilizing readers.

In such a state, the trance state so often alluded to in *Moby-Dick*, feelings are experienced from afar, filtered and abstracted, as though they belong to someone else. The entranced one, like Nabokov's characters driven by voyeuristic impulses that simulate, with exquisite verisimilitude, genuine feelings, watches his feelings, and shapes and directs them, as articles outside himself. Having disowned them, he tells himself they are not his. In time they won't be. The process of separating oneself from one's feelings depends on convincing oneself and others that the feelings are theirs.

In *Moby-Dick* this process spirals outward from the narrator, frozen in euphoria and intent on transmitting his euphoria through his story to readers. Caught between who he feels himself to be, which is intolerable to him, and his sublime image of himself—Ahab, Ahab-awful no less than Ahab-tragic—Ishmael, travelling Voice, disowns himself by disappearing into his Ahab-image. The process continues with Ahab, disowning who he is, an aging, crippled man, by disappearing into sublime imagery of what he wants to be, an egregiously intact, immortal Whale.[3]

Both seek to mesmerize, then seek refuge in the eyes of those they have mesmerized—for Ahab the crew, for Ishmael the reader—in an effort to convince themselves that they are what they claim they are. For Ishmael, in a relation with Ahab that exists solely in fantasy, which means nothing can impair his fusion with his sublime image, Ahab's obsession with Moby-Dick serves the same function as his own obsession with Ahab. Ishmael's Ahab's obsession with the whale keeps Ahab out of his feelings, keeps him, Ishmael, crew and readers in a constant state of apprehension and excitement, and thus enables him—and his creator, Ishmael, who speaks him into existence—to picture themselves invested with an aliveness that makes them more important, with a more important job to do, than other mortals. This is how narcissism in *Moby-Dick*, and narcissistic fusion, overflow site and character and come to constitute the ambience of the book.

The multiple stages of fusion in which Melville, narrator, protagonist and reader become embroiled commence with Ishmael's remarks about Narcissus.

In "Loomings," Chapter One, appears the first sustained example of the narrator's eloquence, beginning as he tells, jauntily, not in past but present tense, that the way he gets rid of his murderous fantasies is by going to sea. The passage climaxes, and this is the climax of the chapter as well, in the reference to Narcissus. The long paragraph is about water, element of Moby-Dick, and how we—all of us, says Ishmael—are drawn to it:

> Why did the old Persians hold the sea holy? Why did the Greeks give it a separate deity, and make him the own brother of Jove? Surely all this is not without meaning. And still deeper the meaning of that story of Narcissus, who because he could not grasp the tormenting, mild image he saw in the fountain, plunged into it and was drowned. But that same image, we ourselves see in all rivers and oceans. It is the image of the ungraspable phantom of life; and this is the key to it all. (14)

Even should we choose to read the passage as Ishmaelian banter, it is not without meaning that, of all the variants of the myth Melville might have picked, he picked this one. In Frazier's version, Narcissus dies on the bank by languishing away.[4] Robert Graves, citing Ovid, gives a variant of the story in which Narcissus stabs himself with a dagger, Tiresias having prophesied that he would live to a ripe old age, "provided that he never know himself."[5] Melville has Narcissus perish by drowning, and the syntax of the passage leaves ambiguous whether he drowns in despair of reaching the image or in pursuit of it.

This too, surely, is not without meaning, since pursuing and ultimately drowning in his image is also how Ishmael implicates readers and urges us to see ourselves as him.[6] Having intimated that going to sea, while it diverts him from thinking about death, also resembles death, even, to him, resembles a form of dying or killing, he also tells us that we—nearly all of us—feel the same way he feels. We just do not, as of yet, know it:

> This is my substitute for pistol and ball...There is nothing surprising in this. If they but knew it, almost all men in their degree, some time or other, cherish very nearly the same feelings towards the ocean with me. (12)

Ishmael, coercive and slippery at the same time, often uses qualifiers like those above. It is a gesture of politeness. Suggesting not that it is everyone but merely most persons, who, not invariably but probably and eventually feel towards the ocean the same way he feels, the narrator portrays himself as judicious and his readers as the free people of a free land. He is also, at such moments, fusing with readers, much as Ahab, in a parallel moment, fuses, persuading the harpooneers, and, through them, the crew: "I do not order ye; ye will it" (146).

By his sheer repetition to the crew that it is not his will they are following but their own, Ahab will bring the men to a state of docility that exceeds obedience and approaches telepathy. So tentative will grow the boundary between them and Ahab, so thoroughly will Ahab's fantasy image of his body—Moby-Dick, unhurtable—imbue their images of their own, and they become virtually sequestered from their own feelings, that even when they quiver with foreboding they will not feel the fear that makes them quiver:

> There she blows! Had the trump of judgment blown, they could not have quivered more; yet still they felt no terror; rather pleasure. For though it was a most unwonted hour, yet so impressive was the cry, and so deliriously exciting, that almost every soul on board instinctively desired a lowering. (200)

It shall become instinctive for the crew to do what Ahab wants them to do, because of the euphoria he transmits to them.

Euphoric identification with a dominant figure, often a figure with the authority to punish, entails experiencing that figure's wishes as one's own, which requires the forsaking of one's own inner life. Again not without meaning, given how the *Pequod* crew's dearth of inner life is consistently romanticized in *Moby-Dick*. Ahab pronounces them, admiringly, "Pagan leopards...unrecking and unworshipping things, that live, and seek, and give no reasons for the torrid life they feel! The crew, man, the crew!" (144) Virtually devoid of individual personality, even of personhood, as they are, it is questionable how members of the crew can feel any life at all, much less life that is "torrid." Perhaps the narrator's own torrid response to Ahab is what prostrates his shipmates with heat, and that is why they become, to a man, utterly compliant, a circumstance Ishmael "weaves round with tragic graces" (114). Unwoven and un-spun, what Ishmael's Ahab's "I do not order ye; ye will it" displays, meticulously, is how obedience can induce excitement and trance, the trance of a deliriously excited, obedient *Pequod* crew. Delirium is contagious, as we see in the passage regarding the lowering that is "instinctively desired." Indeed, contagion, known in *Moby-Dick* as "magnetism," is what keeps it going.[7]

This suggests that the "dread" Ishmael claims to feel as his shout goes up with the others, far from promising a recovery of his will to live, or separating him from Ahab, binds him all the more closely, since the dread not only does not abate but effectually fuels his "wild, mystical, sympathetical feeling" (155). It is the same excited, impotent dread of Starbuck, who will soliloquize, darkly, on the question Ahab plants in his mind: how truly distinct is he or any other member of the crew from Ahab? "Aye, and say'st the men have vow'd thy vow; say'st all of us are Ahabs" (422). The portentous, melodramatic quality of Starbuck's worry is the clue to its hollowness. In the story told by Ishmael, it is as critical for the protagonist Ahab that the crew, including Starbuck, see themselves as Ahabs, heroic-awful, as it is for the narrator that "all of us," his readers, see ourselves as Ishmaels, presumptively judicious and normative. It is necessary for the narrator because under the guise of normative truth essential propagandistic details of his vision work their way into the tale.[8]

Thus, as a normative if esoteric truth, death-by-water arrives in the first chapter of the book, and water becomes the element not of cleansing or feeling or birth, but trickery. By persistently implying that he knows us better than we know ourselves, Ishmael encourages readers to see how—that is, see what—he sees, telling us too, in case it should cross our minds, that in his way of looking at things there is "nothing surprising" (12). It will cross our minds, as the idea of mutiny crosses the minds of the *Pequod*'s crew, but the narrator, by this type of second-guessing his reader, will habitually render pathology as normative, unsurprising, and, at last, scarcely upsetting. That Melville should have Narcissus plunge into the water, then, is fitting, since this act as fully realizes fusing with one's image as it is possible to do, and the compelled endeavor to fade into one's image is what narcissism is about.

It is also about a form of damnation, as in variants of the myth where Narcissus's infatuation with his image represents punishment by the gods for his having rejected the love of the wood nymph, Echo. To hear one's Echo signifies willingness to "hear" one's self. But hearing himself is an act of which Narcissus, enamored with surfaces, is afraid. Dreading and loathing that which has no surface, his Echo, his soul, he is incapable of love and condemned to "narcissism," entrancement unto death with an image of himself.[9] We may read Tiresias' prophecy to mean that the day Narcissus sees his image is the day the image will take him over— just what happens, what has been happening all along, to Ahab, who, hours before his death, peers into the water for the first time on the voyage, and sees not his own reflection but, many fathoms down, beneath a calm surface whose euphoric waves are "suspended" in "exceeding rapture," the "glittering" open mouth of Moby-Dick, "like an open-doored marble tomb"—if not the key to it all, the swallower of it (448).

Ahab sees the White Whale's open mouth because that mouth is what he needs to see, because he is striving to suck from it, as Ishmael strives to suck from Ahab's eloquence, the glittering image which will, they hope, bring them to life. Because the life they seek is not breathing, human life, however, but a controlled simulation in which, like Ahab's ideal man, they do not feel, but choreograph and manuever, performing their feelings, the imagery does not revive, but anaesthetizes.

If this is not what they truly want, then it is, after all, as much as they can handle, for both characters envy and fear, are literally petrified with fright, by anything that is more alive than they are. I spoke earlier of how Ishmael, in his need to conceive his captain as inhuman or superhuman—he makes no distinction—turns Ahab into a statue; Sharon Cameron points out that Ahab is not alone, since aboard the *Pequod* it becomes, in time, routine to look upon one's body not as a living organism but a defensive structure, a stockade, barricade or fort, if not a jail. Aboard the *Pequod*, in fact, emanating from the narrator, subsists a diffuse, pulsating resentment at having to be in a body at all.

This resentment is displaced to his shipmates by Ishmael, whose own angry bewilderment at having to be in his body is an undersong of his tale. The displacement occurs repeatedly. It is traceable in how the narrator ignores his own body and is fascinated by Queequeg's, a fascination heightened by an eerie sense that he cannot quite believe it is a body. It is also traceable in the dismemberments of various sorts that pepper the story, from Queequeg's peddling preserved heads in New Bedford, to Ishmael's discussion in small sections, like a puzzle's pieces, of whale anatomy, to his minute explanations about the butchering of the slaughtered whale. The note of horror that runs through these passages is muted. Sometimes it is jocular, at other times grandiose, but it is always there. What is not there, what does not come to life in the book, is a sense of vital human flesh.

Because the flesh of the human characters is not alive— Queequeg is more alive than anyone, almost as alive as the whales, and it is his very aliveness that Ishmael finds so pleasing and disconcerting—they must fuse with another organism. This too is consonant with traditional psychological theory, according to which the narcissistic person avidly seeks a candidate for fusion so as not to feel his own lack of aliveness, and in the process confuses sublime images of himself with his actual bodily self. For Ahab, accession to the sublime image entails abhoring, killing and thereby magically fusing with the White Whale. For Ishmael, unparented and self-abhoring, accession requires that he find, then lose himself in a Queequeg, preparatory to finding, then losing himself in an Ahab, both of whom he will, at the end of the adventure, kill. Narrator and protagonist, "hunters...namelessly transported," (447) each regard their hate as transport to transcendent forms of love, and regard their "true" selves as higher than, as if detachable from, their bodies, which they look upon as objects to be mastered.

They look down upon themselves, that is, as they look down upon others, secretly, as "things." This looking down, this willed posture of indiscriminate contempt, torments them with guilt—the wellspring of both characters' anguish—which they refuse to feel. But the refusal reemerges and subsists, "inscrutably," wherever they go, a thing unlike any other thing dead or alive, as the lethal white Fate drawing them on and awaiting their arrival at the opposite end of the waters where they embarked.

As the posture grows habitual, the guilt deepens, and so does the imperative to deny it, deny that they are anything other than what they say they are, deny that they are up to anything horrific, or that anything is wrong. They are doing what Claudius is doing the instant he opens his mouth in *Hamlet*.

The narrator of *Moby-Dick*, more a Gertrude than a Claudius, hides from his guilt, which grows with his growing unwillingness to question that with which he is complicit, and fades away from himself into his voice, so as to make what is occurring unreal: "a play of forces." And as his guilt grows, so does his proclivity to see Ahab as a forced thing who cannot help himself, and to see his adventure with Ahab as an experience of thingness and foreboding. From Stubb's early remark about how Ahab's chest, like metal, rings when he beats it, and rings vast but hollow, to the narrator's late comparisons of Ahab to a blasted tree, a black sand beach, a madness maddened, to Ahab's vision of himself as a match and the crew as anthills of powder, from the sheer reiteration of such images, which themselves proceed from Ishmael's resolve not to feel guilty, grows the atmosphere of doom that haunts the book. Haunting it too is his unflagging sentimentality, as when he reminds readers that, although Ahab's chest may ring like metal, he can also emit a "terrific, loud animal sob, like that of a heart-stricken moose (143). The narrator's sentimentality, and the incongruous imagery it engenders, is pure "spin." What is being "spun," and thereby concealed, is the necessity that Ahab sustain the trance state into which he works himself and the crew, which, by keeping them from waking up to what they are doing, will obviate the threat of mutiny.

Ishmael's prescience on this matter suggests that the possibility of his reader's balking or rebelling is no further from the narrator's mind than the threat of mutiny is from the captain's:

> From even the barely hinted imputation of usurpation, and
> the possibile consequences of such a suppressed impression

gaining ground, Ahab must of course have been most anxious
to protect himself. That protection could only consist in his
own predominating brain and heart and hand, backed by a
heedful, closely calculating attention to every minute atmospheric influence which it was possible for his crew to be sub-
jected to. (184)

From early in the book the reader is in the position of Starbuck,
and Ishmael makes clear that Ahab's "calculating attention to
every minute atmospheric influence," while directed at the crew as
a whole, more specifically targets the sensitive first mate, who
believes that Ahab is reading his mind. Starbuck's anxiety that
Ahab may be right, that all of us are Ahabs, partially explains the
vertigo that besets him when he's in Ahab's presence.[10] But Ahab,
aware of the vertigo, uses a brilliant technique to intensify it and
complete his domination of Starbuck: he affects, at dramatic
moments, to confide in the first mate. These moments of fatherli-
ness, of Ahab appearing to treat Starbuck as a favored son, an
Isaac, who can understand, pity and forgive him, even unto death,
enrapture the younger man. So priceless to Starbuck is the little
vulnerability Ahab shows—his asking Starbuck to "brush this old
hair aside," and the one "priceless tear" he weeps—that he, along
with the narrator, essentially forgets his revulsion (443-4). It is by
means of just such moments of seeming to be vulnerable, to take
off his armor, interspersed, strategically, through hours of the
armor's glittering, that Ahab holds Starbuck and the crew in a spell
of fusion vitalized by a "calculating attention" that involves both
guilt and flattery, theater and the rawest need.[11]

Against his will, Starbuck feels recreated when he is near Ahab,
and his thrill, and the narrator's sureness of feeling for whatever
linguistic or tonal shifts are needed to sustain it in a given passage,
is the ambience of the *Pequod*'s retrogressive voyage.[12] Voiced-
over by the fluid, skillful persuader Ishmael, what Starbuck feels is
what the spheres—the True and, until now, Hidden spheres—felt
when they were made: a thrill, Ishmael reveals, not of love, but
fright (169). It is just this thrill of fright, a fright too chronic to be
felt as fright, and felt, therefore, insofar as it is felt at all, at several removes, that pervades the atmosphere of Melville's novel,
where Ahab is represented by the narrator as a force of nature and
the crew as its Divine Inert, earthbound material.[13] By reproducing in this atmosphere, in relation to readers, the posture of Ahab
towards the crew, Ishmael fuses with his audience, and he the narrator and Melville the author become one and indistinguishable.[14]

Appealing to and feeding readers' atavistic longings, or what Lasch, citing Morris Dickstein, calls "archaic elements," the narcissistic writer attracts us to him, daring us to be like him and go with him "toward a passive and primeval state in which the world remains uncreated, unformed...a "dark, wet hole," as Rudolph Wurlitzer writes in Nog" (*Culture,* 12).

The dark, wet mouth of Moby-Dick is treacherous, seductive and scornful. Towards this mouth—the size of which, extending over three-quarters of the whale's length, fascinates Ishmael—the *Pequod* is pulled across three oceans. When the ship finally draws near and Moby-Dick opens his mouth for Ahab, it is as if solely for the delight of showing him how big it is. Such scorn by the twisted, silent, grinning mouth that formerly "dismasted" him, is intrinsic to its pull.[15] Indeed, the White Whale's "scorn," the repository of which is his "scrolled jaw," is why Ahab considers it incumbent upon him, and necessary to his dignity, to pay the Whale back, why he can't wait, why he sleeps with clenched hands and wakes with bloody fists, why "joy and sorrow, hope and fear seemed ground to finest dust...in the clamped mortar of Ahab's iron soul" (438, 448), why he is, and is proud to be, madness maddened.

Moby-Dick's putative scorn is also why Ishmael, with no less keen an appetite for vengeance, does not sound absurd when, in tones of hushed, fateful reverence, he portrays White Whale-hating Ahab in Napoleonic poses, as in his first, indelible vision of his captain: "His bone leg steadied in that hole; one arm elevated, and holding by a shroud; Captain Ahab stood erect, looking straight out beyond the ship's ever-pitching prow" (110). From this image, intended to evoke pity and awe, Ishmael continues. There is not a whisper of scepticism, to say nothing of regret, grief or anger in his voice, only exaltation: "There was an infinity of firmest fortitide, a determinate, unsurrenderable willfulness, in the fixed and fearless, forward dedication of that glance" (111). In a flourish, the editorial clenchers march in: the "crucifixion in his face...the nameless regal overbearing dignity of some mighty woe ...the clouds that layer upon layer were piled upon his brow," but fittingly, adds the soaring narrator, since "all clouds choose the loftiest peaks to pile themselves upon" (111).

Ishmael's seeming critiques of Ahab, which readers anxious to redeem the narrator from collusion with the protagonist so often cite, cannot logically be isolated from this first image. The novel,

we remember again, is in the fictive construct written as a memory, after Ishmael has grown older, and, he implies, and the convention of the past tense implies, wiser. In *Moby-Dick* the first image
of the protagonist Ahab not only does not differ from, but effectually sets the tone for those that ensue. It does not suggest a narrator grown wiser. Rather, the first image, along with subsequent
imagery, quintessentially statuesque and adoring, indicate a narrator not a whit more insightful now than when he sailed aboard the
Pequod. Ishmael has kept the faith. An awe-struck tour guide
escorting readers through a museum of Ahab poses, his is the language not of reflection, but elegy.

But that is how Ishmael has to talk. Fabricating then venerating
iconic imagery of his symbiotic partner is, on the part of Ishmael
the follower, the requisite complement to Ahab's self-satisfied
depictions of himself as a puppet of god, depictions which, far
from suggesting even a nascent awareness by him or by Ishmael of
who he is, represent instead how inured he is to how he has always
been. When Ahab, prancing, asks near the end of the book—
resoundingly, sensationally—"Is Ahab, Ahab?" and announces
that it is God Who "does that beating, does that thinking, does
that living, and not I" (445), he is simply declaring out loud what
formerly he only hinted: that being God's puppet means he is a
chosen vessel. Which is why he can inform Starbuck—"Fool!" and
"underling!"—without embarrassment, to say nothing of fear or
trembling, that he, Ahab, is the "Fates' lieutenant," whose "whole
act's immutably decreed" (459).

Ahab's certitude that he was born to be Destiny's officer, that he
personifies Destiny—which also has it in for him—is his and the
narrator's abiding rationale for each act he commits.[16] It is the
ground of his contempt for other humans, a contempt Ishmael
covertly shares, as evinced in the "Queen Mab" and "Carpenter"
episodes. The reader may yearn in these chapters for the narrator
to give some sign that, in hindsight, at least, he questions, or even
sees, the grotesque content of the scenes he describes. Instead, fad-
ing into his hero, Ishmael demonstrates remarkable complacency,
tolerance and empathy with the fact that Ahab quite openly finds
others despicable. His own contempt is why the narrator in
"Queen Mab," intending no irony whatever, has Stubb raised to
the wisdom of apprehending that the proper response to being
kicked by an Ahab is not anger, but gratitude, because Ahab is a
"great" man: "No, you were kicked by a great man, and with a

beautiful ivory leg, Stubb," says the Humpback of Stubb's dream, the transfigured Moby-Dick:

> ...be *your* boast, Stubb, that ye were kicked by old Ahab, and made a wise man of. Remember what I say; *be* kicked by him; account his kicks honors; and on no account kick back; for you can't help yourself, wise Stubb. (116)

The wry, indefinite timbre of the Humpback's voice does not change the circumstance that Ishmael has Stubb believe him and take his advice seriously, believe Ahab's kick makes him wise, and believe and take solace in the belief that he "can't help" himself.[17] That Ahab has kicked Stubb before, and called him a dog, and can tolerate no frustration other than that involved in his pursuit of the White Whale, does not at any point noticeably discompose the narrator.

Why?

Because Ishmael is excited by the kick and by Stubb's submission to it in the same way he is excited by the numerous other acts of cruelty and submission that move the story forward, because imagery involving cruelty and submission is what brings his voice to life. From his jolly reference to the "universal thump," to his sense of being victimized in various degrees by his landlord, the townspeople of New Bedford, Elijah and Bildad, to the unqualified submission of the crew, particularly Starbuck, to Ahab, to Ahab's own submission to Fedallah, the narrative weaves its way through acts of cruelty which the perpetrator shows no sign of recognizing and the victim does not protest at all, protests weakly, or rescinds his protest.

Genuine protest finds no place in *Moby-Dick* because narrator and protagonist are so utterly preoccupied with an image of sublimity that their tale is often but a context for this preoccupation.[18] Ishmael's veiled narcissism is the grounds of his connivance with, approval and applause of the unabashedly narcissistic Ahab, and is why the nominal measures he takes to conceal his approval collapse, whenever he speaks of Ahab, in the high-pitched euphoria of his voice. He prefers to feel lofty rather than feel ashamed, and that is why, when he imagines the scene between Ahab and the carpenter, his own jollity is as undeterred by Ahab's jovial abuse of the workman as Ahab himself, reflecting on his own magnificence— "Here I am, proud as a Greek god, and yet standing debtor to this blockhead" (391-2)—is undeterred by the carpenter's presence.

Ahab is not embarrassed to preen in front of the carpenter, or
ridicule him to his face, because to Ahab, euphorically-identified
with the White Whale, and to Ishmael, euphorically-identified
with Ahab, the carpenter is not real.

This euphoria is the primary expression of the narcissistic universe portrayed in *Moby-Dick*. When Ishmael is euphoric, and he
is often so, it is because euphoria relieves him of the terror of genuine feeling. Euphoria is what he is after in the mournful, grand,
elegiac tone he adopts as if reflexively when speaking of Ahab, for
in euphoria he ceases to be a "loser" and becomes a "winner,"
untottering, like Ahab, and, like Ahab, lifting his brow to Dawn
for a kiss:

> Tied up and twisted; gnarled and knotted with wrinkles; hag-
> gardly firm and unyielding; his eyes glowing like coals, that
> still glow in the ashes of ruin; untottering Ahab stood forth in
> the clearness of the morn; lifting his splintered helmet of a
> brow to the fair girl's forehead of heaven...(442)

Meanwhile, by the hortatory lilt of his phrasing and the
omnipresent first-person plural—"Oh, immortal infancy, and
innocency of the azure! Invisible winged creatures that frolic all
round us!" (442)—the narrator obscures and finally erases the
boundaries between himself and readers.

Which suggests that a major source of Ishmael's persuasiveness
is his narcissism itself. And indeed, his assumption that his audience, as we read *Moby-Dick*, will under his tutelage learn to
become other Ishmaels, confers upon the narrative considerable
authority, just as the sheer tenacity of Ahab's assumption that the
crew will go along with him and hate Moby-Dick as he does is critical to his success in teaching them to do so. His conviction that he
can by force of will bring the wills of others into what he will represent as harmony with his own—a harmony in which he rules and
they submit—is central to Ahab's charisma, to charisma itself, a
subject which also intrigued Hawthorne, whose *House of Seven
Gables* portrays a situation that underscores the point being made
here.

This is the analogue to the moment in *Moby-Dick* when Ahab
gains ascendancy over Starbuck, which the narrator imagines as
the penetration of Starbuck's lungs and body by Ahab's will:
"Something shot from my dilated nostrils, he has inhaled it in his
lungs. Starbuck now is mine...(144). The corresponding moment
in Hawthorne's novel occurs when Matthew Maule, standing in

the presence of Alice Pyncheon's father, draws the young woman under his power by gazing at her hypnotically. Just as the magnetism of the White Whale's mouth migrates and is reconfigured in the magnetic, sucking force of Ahab's stare, so does Maule's well, the gravitational center of Hawthorne's book, unleash itself from dormancy and become alive in the carpenter's eyes, into which Alice falls and drowns:

> ...Mr. Pyncheon heard a half-uttered exclamation from his daughter. It was very faint and low; so indistinct that there seemed but half a will to shape out the words, and too undefined a purport to be intelligible. Yet it was a call for help!— his conscience never doubted it;—and, little more than a whisper to his ear, it was a dismal shriek, and long reechoed so, in the region round his heart! (*House*, 244)

The vengeful laborer brings Alice under his spell by gazing at her so fixedly that he wrests control of the recesses of her selfhood, specifically of her ability to say no.[19]

Matthew Maule will cause Alice Pyncheon to come and go as he wills, and scenes like this, of one character seizing possession of another through psychic subjugation and humiliation, recur throughout the works of Melville and Hawthorne. Both writers are fascinated by how the charismatic figure, by steadily denying that boundaries exist between himself and other characters, quietly dissolves those boundaries and undermines the other's will to maintain himself as a separate being. But the persuading away of another's separateness, represented in the latter's volition to say no—gestalt psychologists posit a "'no' reflex"—occurs in another dimension as well, that inhabited by reader and writer, and understood in the conventional expression, "suspension of disbelief," which denotes temporary surrender by readers of their volition to say "no" to what they are reading.

In order to simulate a sense of himself as powerful, Ishmael needs simultaneously to imagine the reader as powerless and continually to vanquish potential readerly resistance, just as Ahab needs to see the crew as mere extensions of his will and at the same time be constantly attentive to every atmospheric influence that might inspire them to think otherwise. No one does think otherwise; Ishmael's Ahab has his way with every member of the crew, and the ease with which he has it makes him despise them: "I thought to find one stubborn, at the least; but my one cogged circle fits into all their various wheels, and they revolve" (147).

The next chapter will explore the interesting question of whether Melville, revolving readers, depises us. Before concluding this one, I would like to summarize and entertain some final thoughts regarding narcissism in the novel.

It is because the narcissistic person is unable to see the otherness of other persons except as a threat that he hates them, at the same time that he needs and uses them, and that is why he feels like an imposter. Feeling like an imposter is unbearable, so he must convert his guilt into another, trumped-up feeling. This magical conversion of one's inadequacies into virtues that mark one as superior to other persons becomes more than a habit. It becomes, with practice, a reflex. The narcissist converts his guilt that he is an imposter into its compensatory opposite: nobility.

Upon the idea of nobility Ishmael's tale spirals, the most conspicuous spiralling in the text being the narrator's voice itself. The spiralling, involving, coiling energy that so often invests his syntax, and the breathless, spiralling ecstasy of his voice act on the reader in a manner that duplicates how Ahab's oratory acts on the crew.[20] His erudition, his melancholy, the wealth of his allusions and the elevated tone of his storytelling imply, moreover, that his portrait of Ahab as a sublime rebel is, itself, sublime.

In the reading I am proposing Ahab is not a rebel. He is a hater. His hate produces impressive postures of defiance, and these postures frighten and excite narrator and crew. The strength of the postures, however, comes not from his standing up, an unfractioned, uncompromised integral, against the unfair laws of God and man, though that is what he and the narrator proclaim. Far from it. What Ahab's postures come from is his need to maintain his sublime image of himself. The effect of the narrator's complicity with Ahab is to turn Ahab into the "magnet" to which Ishmael so often compares him.

In proposing that *Moby-Dick* proceeds from a vitiated point of view, a point of view distorted by fear, I have juxtaposed Freudian concepts of narcissism to Ahab and Ishmael to see what would happen. What emerges from this analysis is a narrator who needs and creates an image of what he conceives to be mortal greatness. I have called this image a simulation of a tragic hero, and proposed further that the simulation, the image that looks like a tragic hero, is a narcissist of the pathological order.[21]

I have so far investigated Ishmael, the voice in front of Melville. The next chapter will examine what the fictive narrator's voice may disclose of the author himself.

Notes

1.   The burgeoning academic field of "media studies" has rendered commonplace Christopher Lasch's observation that, "In propoganda, as in advertising, the important consideration is not whether the information accurately describes an objective situation but whether it sounds true" (*Culture*, p. 76). Lasch's remarks regarding the quality of rehearsed self-promotion in much twentieth-century American fiction, and the habit of narrators overtly to display one set of postures towards their readers while covertly, as though in their own shadows, enacting another, suggest that Ishmael is precursor to a brotherhood of later narrators, those of Nabokov, Mailer and Pynchon, to name a few. Lasch's analysis of what may be a particularly American, or "First World" phenomenon—how a citizenry's "sense of endless possibility" can languish and atrophy in "the banality of the social order they have erected against it—" while sweeping, is consonant with psychoanalytic theory, and pertinent to my thesis:

> Having internalized the social restraints by means of which they formerly sought to keep possibility within civilized limits, they feel themselves overwhelmed by an annihilating boredom, like animals whose instincts have withered in captivity. *A reversion to savagery threatens them so precisely them so little that they long precisely for a more vigorous instinctual existence.* People nowadays complain of an inability to feel (*Culture*, p. 11, my italics).

2.   Thomas Weiskel investigates in the aesthetics of Kant and Burke "why a diffuse melancholy predisposes to the sublime." His discussion of "the absence-phase of desire" illuminates important features of the Ishmael-Ahab symbiotic axis (*Romantic Sublime*, pp. 105, 154). So does Kierkegaard's concept of "double-mindedness:"

> For whether the weakling despairs over not being able to wrench himself away from the bad, or whether the brazen one despairs over not being able to tear himself completely away from the Good—they are both double-minded, they both have two wills. Neither of them honestly wills one thing, however desperately they may seem to will it ("Purity of Heart," in *A Kierkegaard Anthology*, pp. 276-7).

3.   Psychoanalyst Theodore Rubin describes the narcissist as one who "becomes his own world and believes the whole world is him;" psychoanalyst Otto Kernberg looks at how his "chronic uncertainty and dissatisfaction about himself" leads to idealized performances in front of others *Narcissism*, p. 6). Lasch, citing Kernberg, writes of how the narcissistic person, feeling his "amorphous existence to be futile and purposeless," accrues "a sense of heightened self-esteem only by attaching himself to strong, admired figures...The narcissist admires and identifies himself with "winners" out of his fear of being labelled a "loser" (*Culture*, pp. 37, 85). Throughout *Our Adult World* Melanie Klein discusses the "splitting" into accepted and rejected aspects.

4.   Sir James Frazier, *The Golden Bough*, p. 192

5.   Robert Graves, *The Greek Myths*, p. 286.

6.   In "How to Make Double-Talk Speak," Carolyn Porter looks at how Ishmael, by speaking "in the name of 'all men'... persistently blurs the very distinctions to which he appeals..." She also discusses "the ironically self-authorizing effects of Ishmael's double-voiced discourse" and "Melville's fear of boundary dissolution" (*New Essays on* Moby-Dick, pp. 73, 79, 98, 106). Jenny Franchot refers to the "polyvocality" in the opening pages of *Moby-Dick* ("Melville's Travelling God, *Cambridge Companion*, p. 171).

7.   Alice Miller, discussing "poisonous pedagogy," cites comparable forms of such delirious excitement, as in Rauschning's remarks concerning the eagerness of those who came into contact with Hitler to bathe and vanish in his "nimbus." This "nimbus," says Miller, and "the early enforcement and suppression of feelings" are the reasons why many a "properly raised child...can never gain any insight" into himself or what has happened to him. She quotes Hitler: "It also gives us a very special, secret pleasure to see how unaware the people around us are of what is really happening to them" (*Good*, pp. 58, 63, 72-75).

In *The Gansevoorts of Albany*, Alice Kenney details the minuteness with which proprieties were observed in the Melville-Gansevoort household. Weaver and Robertson-Lorant write of Allan Melville's need to be seen as "a paragon of propriety—a model of rigid decorum" (*Herman Melville: Mariner and Mystic*, p. 57). Howard writes of the chronic "tensions in the Melville household" (Howard's *Herman Melville*, p. 15). Mumford calls both of the parents "monsters" and suggests that it is precisely because "Melville's mother and father...were correct and meritorious members of society" that it was so hard for him to come to terms with his true feelings about them: "...it is difficult to believe that the image of God can err, if it be repeated often enough" (Mumford's *Herman Melville*, p. 15).

8.   In a brilliant essay, Donald Pease shows how Ishmael's way of writing about Ahab has the effect of legitimizing the narrator himself:

> ...the Ishmael who was taken in by Ahab's rhetoric does not, as was the case with other narrators of the tall tales, use the tale to work through the excesses of Ahab's rhetoric. Instead,

the extraordinary nature of Ahab's words and deeds legit-
imizes elements of Ishmael's narrative that might otherwise
seem inflationary...Ahab turns into the figure who enables the
reader to rule out the charge of excess in Ishmael's rhetoric
(*"Moby-Dick* and the Cold War" in *The American
Renaissance Reconsidered*, p. 145).

9.

His reflection...shows only his perfect, wonderful side and not
his other parts. His back view, for instance, and his shadow
remain hidden from him...This stage of rapture can be com-
pared with grandiosity, just as the next (the consuming longing for himself) can be likened to depression.
Narcissus...denied his true self, wanting to be at one with the
beautiful picture (Miller, *Drama*, p. 49).

Lowen suggests that in rejecting Echo, Narcissus is rejecting his own
"inner being...The word "Personality" reflects this idea. Persona means
that by his or her sound you can know the person" (*Narcissism*, p. 27).

10.   Pease deconstructs Ahab's "charisma" as follows:

...Starbuck now feels all the rage he needs to kill Ahab. When
Starbuck feels this, Ahab has him precisely where he wants
him, in a state of mind enabling him to identify Ahab's rage
with an impulse in his own inner life...Ahab "acts out" that
inner life as his means of dominating the Starbuck who
becomes "free" to deny this rebellious will in himself by wit-
nessing it already thoroughly acted out in Ahab...That Ahab
says all this in cadences borrowed from Shakespeare only
underscores the "scenic" character of his separation from the
crew. If he talks to the men at all, he talks...in a language that
immediately encloses him in a theatrical scene ("Cold War,"
p. 143).

11.   A number of scholars, including Bezanson and Milder, make the
analogy to Nazism, but always couched in the assumption that Melville is
criticizing Ahab. In a paper presented before the Melville Society in 1986
and cited by Herbert Mitgang in the *New York Times*, Professor
Christopher S. Durer of the University of Wyoming discusses the "atmospheric influence" aboard the *Pequod* by which

Ahab brings about a state of identification between himself
and the crew...Ahab wants the crew to join in the chase of the
White Whale and devote all their energies to this purpose, but
he does not issue orders. Instead he is trying to create in them
a state of mind in which they themselves will want what he
wants.

Mitgang adds, "The hallmarks of Nazism—propaganda, emotionalism, paganism, psychological enslavement, death to the enemies of the state—are all anticipated in the novel." (*New York Times*, August 26, 1986, Section e, p.13).
In *Mariners, Renegades and Castaways*, C.L.R. James looks at how Ahab seizes on a one-size-fits-all "program" to solve every ill and right every wrong.
Blau, drawing on David Brion Davis' *Homicide in American Fiction*, p. 111, says that "In Ahab the impulse to love is bound up inseparably with the impulse to murder" (*The Body Impolitic*, pp. 88, 105).

12.   Some readers have remarked, with fervid awe from which even the ghost of any poor spirit of inquiry has fled, the sense of excitement they get from *Moby-Dick*. Arvin calls it "expanded personal force." For Berthoff,

> ...at the heart of Melville's power to persuade, is the sureness
> of his feeling for what is needed at any given point...To come
> into the presence of such a writer is to experience a broaden-
> ing of apprehension and—perhaps even more important—a
> positive strengthening of capability. We are tempted, indeed,
> to live in his work vicariously (*The Example of Melville*, p.
> 209).

Which is my point.

13.   Citing Toland's biography of Hitler, Alice Miller discusses "the narcissistic, symbiotic unity between Fuhrer and Volk," much romanticized by both. According to his boyhood friend, August Kubizek, before whom Hitler liked to rehearse his speeches, the symbiosis resulted from the state of exaltation Hitler went into when he had an audience:

> "These orations, usually delivered when they were walking
> through the fields...reminded Kubizek of an erupting volcano.
> It was like a scene on the stage. 'I could only stand gaping and
> passive, forgetting to applaud...He always sensed my reac-
> tions as intensely as if they were his. Sometimes I had the feel-
> ing that he was living my life as well as his own'" (*Good*, p.
> 176).

14.   Readers surmise with good reason that Ishmael speaks for Melville. Brodtkorb calls Ishmael "the vessel that contains the book...he is the book (*Ishmael's White World*, pp. 3-4). Bezanson says the narrator is Melville writing "Under the ambiguously sacred name of Ishmael..." ("*Moby-Dick*: Document, Drama, Dream, *A Companion*, p. 187). Parker and others, including contributors to *New Essays on* Moby-Dick, published in 1986, suggest that Melville, in Edwin Miller's words "saw himself as a wounded Narcissus, an Ishmael" (*Melville*, p. 104). Miller discusses the numerous Narcissus figures in Melville's books, and the writer's early interest in the Ishmael figure (pp. 55, 67, 115).

15.   The double, shifting aspect of Moby-Dick's gender is often remarked by readers. In dim Biblical apocrypha associated with German High Criticism, with which Melville was almost certainly familiar, Moby-Dick's ancestor is also suspect on this score:

> The opinion of Izchakis that Jonah was first swallowed by a male fish, and that because he did not pray in it, he was vomited up and swallowed by a female one, in which his situation was more confined, and that from this circumstance he was driven to prayer, deserves mention at best as a curious and warning example of the absurdity to which adherence to the letter may lead in exegesis (Paul Kleinert, "The Book of Jonah," trans. Charles Elliott, in John Peter Lange, *A Commentary on the Holy Scriptures*,p. 25).

Dahlberg writes that "Leviathan in the Zohar is feminine," and that Melville committed sodomy "as it is meant in the Old Testament; in his mind he had had connection with a beast of the deep" (*Alms*, p. 139). Tolchin discusses the "increasing cross-gender identification" that sometimes occurs during a conflicted mourning process, and suggests that Maria Melville reverberates in the character of Ahab:

> Although Ahab's identification with Maria Melville's grief is kept on the novel's margins, it momentarily breaches the surface in "The Candles," where Ahab...claims for himself a "'queenly personality'" (*Mourning*, pp. 34, 118).

Edwin Miller says she reverberates in Mrs. Glendenning, the mother figure of *Pierre*, whom Miller calls a "phallic woman." In the tradition of the earlier biographers, starting with Weaver and continuing with Mumford, Howard, Chase, Stone, Arvin and Robertson-Lorant—the exceptions are Gilman and Parker—Miller sees the relationship between Herman and his mother as disastrous, principally due to her coldness and domineering ways. He says that Maria Melville's neighbors in Pittsfield named her after the Dickens' character, "Mrs. Pecksniff" (Miller's *Melville*, p. 80).

16.   Lowen considers narcissism in a spectrum, the Ahab band of which he denominates the "psychopathic:"

> ...psychopathic personalities consider themselves superior to other people and show a degree of arrogance that verges on contempt for common humanity...They will lie, cheat...even kill, without any sign of remorse...[demonstrating also] an inability to contain frustration. One could regard this weakness as an expression of infantilism in the personality, but I believe it has a different meaning and origin, reflecting the deficient sense of self. One must remember that in other respects—namely in their ability to manipulate people, organ-

ize and promote schemes, and attract followers—narcissistic characters and pysychopathic personalities are anything but infantile (*Narcissism*, p. 23).

17.   Alice Miller, citing Fest's biography of Hitler, notes the propensity of dictators to represent themselves as remote, inscrutable statues sternly looking down upon their subjects, who obligingly look up in awe.

> All through his life he made the strongest efforts to conceal as well as to glorify his own personality...The image he had of himself was more that of a monument than of a man. From the start he endeavored to hide behind it (*Good*, p. 186).

18.   In "*Moby-Dick* as Sacred Text," Lawrence Buell uses Robert Richardson's term "mythic investiture" to describe Melville's novelistic technique in *Moby-Dick*. In Buell's reading Melville makes the White Whale a god whom Ahab envies (*New Essays*, p. 59).

19.   Edgar Dryden, looking at this passage, offers the following interpretation:

> As we have seen, Hawthorne's characters find themselves in a threatening world where the primary danger comes from the gaze of other people. One expression of that danger is "the witchcraft of Maule's eye" (CE 11, 189) which allows the carpenter to "look into people's minds" and "to send them, if he pleased, to do errands to his grandfather, in the spiritual world" (189-190). All of the Maules, including Holgrave, recognize the power of the gaze and use it against others before others can employ it against them. This is the meaning of Holgrave's story of Alice Pyncheon. She seals her fate when she casts an "admiring glance" (201) at Matthew Maule, for he recognizes the threat her gaze poses to his own subjectivity: "Does the girl look at me as if I were a brute beast?" thought he, setting his teeth. "She shall know whether I have a human spirit, and the worse for her if it prove stronger than her own" (201). Because his will is stronger, he drains Alice of her inwardness in the same way she has unconsciously threatened his (*The Poetics of Enchantment*, p. 68).

20.   The language Ishmael gives to Ahab claims for him, writes Pease, "all the "unapproachable" cultural power that Melville, in his review of Hawthorne, claimed Shakespeare wielded over the mob" ("Cold War," p. 143).

21.

> ...his acting is convincing because he himself has become convinced. He identifies with his image, and this becomes his only reality; he no longer senses that he is distorting or denying the truth. In effect, he denies or ignores the reality of his

being, but the denial is no longer deliberate or conscious. The actor has become so identified with his role that it has become real for him (*Narcissism*, p. 55).

In her 1993 poem, "Innocence: 1945," Adrienne Rich writes,

"The beauty of it was the guilt...The guilt made us feel innocent again."

Chapter 3

Seduction

The idea entertained in this chapter is that Melville's fantasy of his reader is central to the book's compelling force.

In proposing that there is a reader whom the writer unconsciously fantasizes, and that this reader affects the atmosphere of a work of fiction, I am not speaking of the fictive reader as developed by theorists of the past three decades.[1] The fictive reader, implied or characterized, is a figure who inhabits the text. The character of Bulkington, for example, might represent the ideal implied reader of *Moby-Dick*, while the lounging aristocrats of the "Town-Ho" chapter, with their persistent need to classify experience, might represent the type of reader of whom Melville is not fond.

The reader whom the writer fantasizes does not inhabit the text, but its emotional envelope.[2] Writers, in other words, do not write blindly, to no one, or to someone without a face. There is a face, or faces, in the text, and fiction, thus considered, is an indirect form of address to these faces, which are the writer's images of his reader. What the writer tells, beside his story and through it, are his fantasies of his reader, himself and their relation.[3]

A primary source of the power in *Moby-Dick* is that, figuratively speaking, Melville's eyes never leave the reader's, any more than Ahab's eyes, especially when he is not looking, ever leave the crew's.[4] In so doing—watching without looking—Ahab is ratifying the compact he strikes with crew members, a cruder version of the same compact Melville makes with readers. It is the anaesthetizing power in this look, a power that derives not from his seeing them but from their seeing in his eyes, whether he is absent or present to them, a stunning image, his image not of them but of himself through them—fearless, questionless—that seduces, then fuses them to him.

Through Ishmael we observe this look in Ahab on occasions when he subdues mates and crew by exciting then bullying them. It is in Ahab's eyes when he enlists the dazzled harpooneers' allegiance to the chase, when he nails up the gold doubloon, and when Ishmael sees him for the first time.

The narrator follows the look and dwells wherever it dwells.[5] It arouses him. Listening to himself talk about it quickens and frightens him, and his language turns spellbinding, like Ahab's glaring eyes themselves. Indeed the intensity of language that pours from Ishmael when he speaks of the look in Ahab's eyes stirs him to life as no other event in the story, not even the most dramatic scenes of fighting with whales, manages to do. For the narrator the look is a narcotic. It invests him, as he talks about it, with a will of its own cognate with the will of Ahab:

> ...that purpose, by its own sheer inveteracy of will, forced itself against gods and devils into a kind of self-assumed, independent being of its own. Nay could grimly live and burn, while the common vitality to which it was conjoined, fled horror-stricken from the unbidden and unfathered birth. (175)

Thus Ishmael portrays the birth of Ahab's Mission—which the narrator denominates "purpose"—a ghastly virgin birth, and speaks too, excitedly, of how it takes him over:

> Therefore, the tormented spirit that glared out of bodily eyes, when what seemed Ahab rushed from his room, was for the time but a vacated thing, a formless, somnambulistic being, a ray of living light, to be sure, but without an object to color, and therefore a blankness in itself. (175)

Equating, as is his custom, intense thought with maniacal possession, he now metaphorically equates Ahab, eating himself up with hate, with Prometheus, punished for giving fire, one of the signs of incipient civilization, to humankind. The narrator is soaring far too high to notice the preposterous character of his metaphor. He soars on, insinuating, by the public, communal quality of his prayer, that he is speaking not on his own behalf, but ours:

> God help thee, old man, thy thoughts have created a creature
> in thee; and he whose intense thinking thus makes him a
> Prometheus; a vulture feeds upon that heart forever; that vul-
> ture the very creature he creates. (175)

The real vulture here, obscured in the narrator's metaphor, is
Ishmael's Ahab's appetite for vengeance. That is what glares out of
his Ahab's eyes. Later the vulture will be the prairie wolf. In the
end it will be Moby-Dick. This, the predacious look in his eyes, is
the instrumentality by which Ahab entrances the crew. But while
Ahab's "blankness in itself" is visible to readers only on those
occasions when Ishmael makes Ahab himself visible (though it is
omnipresent in the atmosphere of the ship, like Fedallah, who
"fixes" Ahab with the same blank look, is omnipresent), the look
Melville, through his narrator, fixes on readers, is at work on every
page. This look is the source of the novel's recurrent trance
imagery, the tracing of which suggests a dynamic between the
writer and his readers of euphoria and possession.[6]

Let us go all the way: the horrified, tantalized reader of *Moby-
Dick* participates in energies which, according to Melville's biographers, characterized the two most intense, painful relationships
of his life, that with his mother and that with Hawthorne, to
whom the book is dedicated.[7] The energies are those of seduction,
thrill and guilt, of manipulation, counter-manipulation and punishment, of constant anticipation of the loss of love, of futile, terrified efforts to fuse, and, above all, of doom.[8]

In an atmosphere possessed, untouchable and strange, pervad-
ing a shorescape itself possessed and euphoric, and a "tormented
sea" afraid of what lives in its depths and transmitting its fear to
whatever ventures upon its surface, the author importunes the
beautiful, unloving faces of Nathaniel Hawthorne and Maria
Gansevoort (201). Like the Gorgon's face, like Moby-Dick's, like
Yahweh's, like those of fairy tale, these faces cannot be besought
directly, and if seen bring death. Melville's curse is the anguished
form of his worship.

The author's curse is his protest at being incarnate. His protest
at being incarnate may begin to explain the spell that binds ani-
mate organisms in his novel, may explain why all undergo a slow
simplification into wax figures, and why the portrayal of life in
Moby-Dick is weirdly altered to a fevered, careful, exhausted pan-
tomime.[9]

Ishmael, without wanting to, is hearkening back to the only world he knew, and replicating it: its still, unbreathing, simulated character, its unreality. The narrator fears that what he fled is following him, and he is correct. Revulsion, paralysis, a sense of time in suspension, of anxious, hopeless waiting, migrates from one object to the next. Rippling outward from the realm of the organic, lifelessness, in the form of somnambulistic imagery, passes into the inorganic and becomes the face of nature itself.[10]

'Lifelessness' may seem an odd word for such a work as *Moby-Dick*, with some of the jauntiest, most aggressive prose in English. But vitality in literature is conveyed not only by the words on the page but the impulse associated with them, an impulse that in Melville's novel seems to thrust the story before it as if to fend it off, a belligerent impulse which, if it could speak, might describe itself like Ahab describes himself, as "pushing, and crowding, and jamming" itself on (444-5). Increasingly, as the story continues, the characters of *Moby-Dick*, pushed and crowded on, move with the stylized equanimity of figures in a trance, deadened to any feeling but that of being mesmerized, which is not feeling but abstraction from feeling. The abstraction emanates from the narrator. It is Ishmael's abstraction from his own feelings, belying his excited prose, that converts the whale hunt to a masque, and gives rise to his impulse to flatten and dull, an impulse which, even in the most beautiful moments of the tale, those, for instance, that have to do with vistas of water and sky, imparts an effect of stage scenery.

In this manner, through a series of mesmerized and mesmerizing scene sets, *Moby-Dick* enacts itself, as though itself in reenactment, ushered in by "silent sentinels all around the town," "crowds, pacing straight for the water, and seemingly bound for a dive," and an "absent-minded" man with whom readers are urged to test the narrator's theory: "...stand that man on his legs, set his feet a-going, and he will infallibly lead you to water" (12-13). He will, of course, that man, since, half-joking though Ishmael's tone is, the quality of movement he ascribes to the man is less a dreamer's than a robot's. The jocular aspect, as well as the Protagorean reasoning—everyone is drawn to water because water draws everyone to it—comes, we remember, after the narrator tells us there is nothing surprising in his death wish, and that most of us share it (12).

We are implicated in the first paragraph of the first chapter, and the spell into which we, through the narrator, are drawn, is elaborated shortly when Ishmael informs readers how a painter, any painter, sees a landscape: it presents itself in a supine posture, "tranced," and in need of a shepherd with eyes "fixed" on a stream (13). Why even landscapes can't escape but have got to "lie tranced," why shepherds cannot just enjoy gazing at streams but must have their eyes "fixed," is because this narrator needs to have it so, because the eyes of most of the characters, most of the time, are "fixed," sightless, because most of the time they are on or near water, and water represents to him a surrender of the will to live.

It is not that Ishmael, in going to sea, is choosing to be destroyed. Rather, it is that it does not much matter to him whether he lives or dies. In this "spell" of apathy, he abdicates the will to choose to see. For spellbound the narrator is: fixed eyes, the eyes of Narcissus staring into the water, exaggerated stillness strangely lacking in repose, and movement not chosen but driven, cast the "spell" to which he succumbs as he watches Queequeg pray to Yojo, the "spell" in which he lay in terror with the supernatural hand in his, the "eternal, unstirring paralysis" of Adam, who Ishmael fancies not dead but "antique," permanently stuck in a "deadly, hopeless trance" (30, 33, 41).

The repetitive trance imagery, mantric and impersonal, is a principal feature of the thrill to which the author invites readers. It is a thrill suggestive of unholy secrets, in the throes of which we seem to be initiated into forbidden mysteries. Adam's "trance" is a major mystery. So is the whiteness of Lima, which "keeps her ruins for ever new" (168). Both are presented by Ishmael as pieces of a momentous, hitherto undisclosed hermetic puzzle. His voyage on the *Pequod* is a mystery too, a privileged, bold, ritualistic incursion into taboo dimensions where we must go incognito, like him, a new Gilgamesh, on our way to revelations until now unspeakable. In the character of revelations, in a hushed voice, the narrator offers cryptic intimations to readers, and, by making us privy to shadow he avows is more real than substance, flatters us and whets our appetite for more.

The most unholy secret into which we will be initiated is that of the uncertain demarcation between what is alive and what is not. In this respect, antique Adam and the "rumor of a knocking in the tomb" are primary, germinative features of the imagination behind *Moby-Dick* (41). They are also clues to the most frightening unconscious fantasy the novel enacts: if the dead do not really die, then perhaps the living are not really alive.

This fantasy, centered on the White Whale, constitutes the "little lower layer" of the revelation of Nature's essential perfidy. Through steadily-flowing imagery of enchantment, which casts a luscious, dream-like color over the tale, *Moby-Dick* hints that the firmest boundary of all, between nonlife and life, is unstable.

Such a hint, and the aura of horror surrounding it, are deeply intriguing.[11] Assiduously the narrator elaborates the intrigue, the sea metamorphosing to the "trance of the sea" and the ship to the "tranced ship" so often that we and he himself will scarcely notice that ship and sea, in an atmosphere of suspended animation, become subject to the same retribution as the human characters (137, 242).

For retribution, exciting, murderous and certain, is what the trance will lead to, and what feeds the narrative excitement. It casts a spell in the air, "enchanted," and over the waves, "gored," "malicious," "exulting" and "vindictive," through which the "vengeful," "burning" *Pequod* thrusts her "vindictive" bows and "urn-like prow," before which space itself seems "vacating itself of life" (241, 97, 264, 450, 353, 201). Everything, not excepting the elements themselves, is recruited. Everything, become an Ahab, reflecting Ahab, enlists in Ahab's quest, represented by the narrator as tragic, to find an object commensurate to his grievance.

The object sought with such fervor is, as in any such quest, found: a "wall" that is also a "monster," the lure by which Ahab entices the crew and Melville, through Ishmael, entices readers (141, 144, 146, 201). It glitters in the gold doubloon, this lure, and beckons in Ahab's "magnetic" question and "magnetic" look, at which no one can look back, and in his "aspect," which, like Moby-Dick's, is "mystic," causing all who behold him to become instantly "petrified" (418). Punishment and the threat and thrill of it so permeate the tale that humblest objects get anointed and made apprenticed sorcerers:

> But in his joy at the enchanted, tacit acquiescence of the mate,
> Ahab did not hear his foreboding invocation; nor yet the low
> laugh from the hold; nor yet the presaging vibrations of the
> winds in the cordage; nor yet the hollow flap of the sails
> against the masts, as for a moment their hearts sank in. (144)

Why, when even Starbuck, the last best hope, is struck by enchantment of Ahab, do the hearts of the personified sails sink? Because (it is no secret) they know what is going to happen.

And, I am suggesting, because the dreadful, unconscious fantasy that being alive, being made to be alive, is punishment, constitutes the psychological core of the revelation *Moby-Dick* purports to offer. We, along with the rest of the created world, were made—outrageously—against our will and without being asked. That is what narrator and protagonist already know. And it is what the crew of the *Pequod*, the sea birds that follow, and the Pacific Ocean itself are finding out.

And whom can they blame?

Their Enemy.

Their—Our—Mutual Enemy is the reason why the natural world as portrayed in this book is a tortured, enchanted, frozen fury, possessed by the need to punish in return.[12]

The need is masked as a dare, Ahab's open invitation to fight back, based on his awakened suspicion, his incontrovertible certainty, that Creation holds him, holds all of us—for the Enemy Is EveryMan's—in contempt. "Unmasking," as Ishmael will spin it, the Enemy's Agent—the White Whale—whom he declares in revelatory language to be the Ur-Enemy's earthly representative, Ahab will punish the Punisher, and rise above the ignominious condition of being scorned by "heaping" scorn back.

The ambience of punishment in *Moby-Dick* is far more, that is, than the conceit of an attenuated Gothicism.[13] Creaking masts and flapping sails deliver warnings, and the crew members grow amorphous and alike, because the *Pequod*, no less than its human crew, is a prop in the service of a restless, anguished, narcissistic need. The need is a contest between the vulnerable "true" self, which knows that it has sold out to an image, suppresses its knowledge and feels terror and guilt, and the wily, exhilarated "false" self, insusceptible to guilt, and determined, whatever the cost, to win.

It will win.[14] The narrator, who despises his "true," feeling self, will let it. In such a contest, emotional deadening will go hand-in-hand with trance imagery, as one denial of feeling prepares the way, rationalizes, and hardens into the next. Thus, after Stubb is humiliated by Ahab, denies his feeling of humiliation, and submits to Ahab, he sees with satisfaction, if not glee, that Ahab has "fixed" Starbuck too, an observation that helps him deny any lingering unease he may feel about his own cowardice (149).

The dismissal of unease is, of course, the price of admission to the spell.[15] Stubb, by his example, is teaching his fellow crew mem-

bers how to pay it. But they are not his only pupils. He is teaching
readers too, for it is not only Ahab holding out a promise to the
crew, but Melville holding out a promise to readers that through
the power of his voice he will lift us to dimensions of ourselves that
have until now been inaccessible, dimensions of untapped power.
There is untapped power in occult secrets, trance and inititation,
power all the more thrilling should it have to do with exposing
pernicious secrets about matters we may have thought we understood. One such matter is the color white, steeped as this is in asso-
ciations the opposite of secrecy. But readers are about to find out
how wrong we were, as we become initiated into the "secret of the
spell" of the white albatross, the "fixed trance of whiteness" on a
Western prairie in winter, the "incantation of this whiteness" that
sends Ahab into "trances of torments" (165, 168, 169, 174).

The deepening trance of torment in *Moby-Dick* associates
with whiteness that female aspect of personality which the narrator seeks to efface in protagonist, and author seeks to efface in
both. We are approaching the climax, delivered in language of a
hieratic and revelatory character, of what Ahab and the narrator
came to teach.

It has "been hinted," says Ishmael, opening the novel's central
chapter in the anonymous, communal passive voice, what Moby-
Dick did to Ahab (163). Now the narrator will reveal what Moby-
Dick did to him—and might have done to us, had we been there:
he, and, for considerations about to be set forth, we ourselyes, but
for fortune, could have been in Ahab's boot(s).

What the whale did...was...be White!

It was his...Whiteness!!! (we're now in the telltale, tellall heart)
the "vague, nameless horror" of his whiteness! "which could not
but occasionally awaken in any man's soul some alarm" (163).

Any man.

Granted, concedes Ishmael, we are used to associating the
color white with "whatever is sweet, and honorable, and sublime"
(164). Yes. But what do we really feel about it? What have we really felt all along?

What we—"most men," at least, even if "few perhaps were
entirely conscious...and therefore may not be able to recall" what
they really felt, and feel—still, what we, they and everyone else
really feels about the color white, Ishmael reveals, is appalled
(167).

If we do not remember we're appalled, he will remind us, teasing and daring us to do what "no man" has done before: "follow" him into "these halls" where "subtlety appeals to subtlety" (167). Once we've followed, and have been sufficiently subtled, we will remember what we nearly forgot: we're so appalled by whiteness that, in point of fact, nothing on this earth appalls us more: "It cannot well be doubted...Nor can it be questioned..." this "rather vague, nameless horror..." this "certain nameless terror ...this crowning attribute of the terrible...the common, hereditary experience of all mankind" (163, 165-6).

Whiteness is "her"—Nature's—crowning attribute of the terrible because within it "there yet lurks an elusive something," an "indefiniteness," a "dumb blankness, full of meaning" (164, 169). Ishmael divulges more. Eventually, by the peroration of the discourse, all colors of the rainbow and all pigmentations whatsoever, have become sly, slick, "subtile deceits...only laid on from without"—while whiteness is revealed to be nothing less than the apocalyptic "unmasked" truth of Nature, which the narrator refers to as feminine and represents as not just "blank," but blank on purpose.

Nature, hand-in-glove with Whiteness, is blank on purpose because She's up to something.

She may fool the others. She does not fool Ishmael, Ahab or Melville, however.

They've found out what She's up to.

They've found out that Whiteness *is* Nature.

They have discerned, furthermore, that Nature is a sinister, diabolical, murderous tease, which it is their duty to expose.

The tease, memento of an ancient, an immemorial Enemy, elicits within us, if we are honest about it, and admit it, like the narrator does, bottomless fear. Our fear of our Enemy Whiteness is not only bottomless, but instinctive and universal. We—all of us— know that White is our Enemy in the same way a young colt, any young colt, in Vermont, who's never seen a buffalo, knows that buffalos are his enemy, and rears with terror if he so much as smells a robe made of buffalo hide.

The Delphic revelation of the teasing Enemy places readers into an alliance with Melville parallel to the alliance between Ishmael and the crew, and Ahab. Ahab, too, purports to reveal to his captivated audience a supernatural tease, and awaken them to their buried, natural, inexhaustible resentment. To Ishmael through Ahab, and to readers through Ishmael, is declassified, unsealed and laid bare the hitherto top-secret Truth about Nature: the smug, insulting, guileful fraud of her "virgin" whiteness, detectable, for true detectives, everywhere, in everything, since from true detectives no suspect, so long as it's white, be it white bear, white shark, white steed (or white mouse) can hide its true face's true expression: "dumb gloating" (164).

It is this "gloating" that Ahab finds insufferable. Ishmael finds it insufferable too, and exhorts readers to rouse ourselves and suffer the insufferable along with him and Ahab, without delay— "Bethink thee of the albatross"! (164).

We'd better rouse ourselves. More to the point, Ishmael had better rouse us, since, "ineffable" though the horrible white gloating is, so much so that he "almost despair[s] of putting it in comprehensible form," much less "analyz[ing]" it, which "would seem impossible," there are no two ways about it (163, 166). Either the narrator makes his case that Nature is White, and Whiteness is "gloating," and convinces readers to take him seriously, and not laugh, or spit, or "else all these chapters might be naught" (163).

The worst thing a reader can do regarding how upset Ishmael is by Whiteness is laugh. For the crusade represented in the chapters of *Moby-Dick* not to be naught, readers must not laugh. To the contrary: we must be roused, which means we must take the narrator's overweening suspicion that Whiteness is gloating at Ahab, him and us as seriously as he does. Considered in this light, "The Whiteness of the Whale," the "hint" become a battle cry, is a mystical, revelatory treatise of outrage at a God Whose principal activity is gloating, and Who has created a universe so that He has a spectacle commensurate with His capacity to gloat. It is also an injunction to readers to wake up and face the fact that this is their Creator, hiding in the body and eating at the heart of life: this teasing, gloating, charming Demon.

Everyone knows, anyway, deep down, even if they don't want to, like Starbuck, or don't remember, like "most men," about the Demon: "without dissent this point be fixed" (166). The narrator cannot remind us often enough. In fact, if we and Starbuck were honest, it wouldn't be Ishmael telling us the awful truth, but us telling him: "Tell me..."! he admonishes (169). Thus, disappearing into readers, the narrator invokes our "common, hereditary experience," presumes what "no man can deny," and discourses in the first-person plural of "the hidden cause we seek," of what "we" have solved, and how "we," through him, are made sadder but wiser (166-7, 169). We *will* be wiser, as he, in the capacity of hierophant, exalts and numbs himself, burying his terror of the teasing Demon in exhilaration at talking about it, like a frightened child in a funhouse excited, then enchanted, by the sound of his own screams.

It is because Melville is so frightened that Ishmael's terror appears at a remove, and the "The Whiteness of the Whale" resembles an inspired incantation. Here, as in many other passages throughout the book, the trance imagery creates effects whose sheer linguistic beauty may send readers, listening to the narrator listen to himself, soaring. The spell that gradually, quietly conquers each element, as Ishmael entrances and etherializes his world, evokes in us too, perhaps, an unusual sense of surrender, of being, albeit vicariously, overcome. His voice, charismatic and relentless, may get under our skin.

If so, it may be because *Moby-Dick* is a defensive work, the work of a wounded and armored sensibility intent on making readers partners in its grievance. To this sensibility Nature is a vengeful, spell-binding tease, and the narrative strategy of revenge is to offer a spell-binding tease of its own. For the spell to work, potential readerly ambivalence must be overcome, as the "half-mutinous" cry of the crew in "The Candles" is overcome, completely. The steady erosion of whatever resistance the crew initially feels, and the nature of the compact they strike, is traceable and quite clear, and what happens to readers in relation to Melville is prefigured with astonishing exactitude in what happens to crew and narrator in relation to Ahab. With an "incantation of revelry" punctuating their growing collective silence, individual members, surrendering one by one to Ahab, signify that they accept the fantasy he offers. They become just what he requires, utterly submissive, while in their fantasies they metamorphose into him, and, by a species of spiritual osmosis, participate in his mystical power: Tashtego stretches forth his hand "like a wand," Stubb's appearance on deck acts "like a charm upon the crew," and the ship itself radiates "charms" (186, 189, 275).

The compact explains why, in the guilty psyche governing the novel, seduction is synonymous with deceit, and deceit with revenge, all concentrated in the ever-present spirit-spout, "for ever alluring us on...treacherously beckoning us on and on ...into this tormented sea, where guilty beings transformed into those fowls

and these fish, seemed condemned to swim on everlastingly..."
(200-1). Seduction is as inescapable as punishment is everlasting,
even for the poor fish. It is the quality of the atmosphere, seduction and an appetite to harm: "the weather, in which, beneath all
its blue blandness, some thought there lurked a devilish charm"
(201). Nature, sentient, immitigable and wily, intends to trick and
humiliate. Her intention is everywhere, infecting everything,
detected by certain unnamed members of the crew, says Ishmael, in
the very air they breathe.

Melville, through Ahab, through Ishmael, is bearer of this revelation. Majestically, gravely, reluctantly! with a hint that he'd
rather be doing something, anything else, if only he could! he, dif-
fident prophet, bares to readers, as Ahab bares to the crew,
Nature's secret viciousness, at work especially—dangerously!—in
just those places we least suspect: "every stately or lovely embla-
zoning—the sweet tinges of sunset skies and woods; yea, and the
gilded velvets of butterflies, and the butterfly cheeks of young
girls" (170).

What are the butterfly cheeks of young girls *really*? We are
about to be told.

Unveiling as awesome mystery, and proclaiming as solemn,
preternatural oracle, Ishmael, frightened and aroused, will tell, for
he knows.

He may arouse in readers a preternatural suspicion about the
answer, since what he knows we know too, and have known all
along, despite ourselves, anyway: "deified Nature," once stripped,
is not only purposely blank, indefinite, guileful, gloating and
white, but grotesquely "palsied." She's so ill She can't stand up,
but "lies before us like a leper." When properly cross-examined,
though, She'll confess what She's been up to and what She is: a
whore who "paints," setting a trap for a john (170).

The trap, which She not merely relatively but "absolutely
paints," is the colored "pasteboard mask" she wears—has to
wear!—to procure her customers. The mask's the thing. She'd have
no customers without it. They would see what She is and run
away. Now, though, Ishmael will make her take it off. Now her
victims will see what she's been hiding: that "little lower layer" of
the White and Ugly—"the charnel-house within," the deified
whore's True Face—to which the text persistently points (170).

Wonder we then at the fiery hunt?

Ishmael, beleaguered wringer of the confession, remover of the mask, detective, is no fonder of whores than of Husseys who manage inns, stepmothers, or girls with butterfly cheeks. All are in the employ of the brothel, Nature. All, then, are out to trick him, not least the subtle, intriguing, hideously beautiful White Whale, horrible not only because he's White and probably divine-demonic—divine *is* demonic—but also because he may be, or able to make himself, female. Ahab worries about this too, nagged by a suspicion that the White Whale may be, if not a god, then an ancillary goddess, Special Agent of the Vengeful Goddess Herself.

For a narrator and protagonist convinced that Nature has designs on them, it is difficult to conceive a more dismal state of affairs. If Moby-Dick is, occasionally, ambiguously, female, then she is, indubitably, a harlot, will, without doubt, try to seduce, and will use seduction to disguise her malice.

She won't succeed, though. Not this time. Her come-uppance is at hand.

Ishmael's Ahab's task is clear.

Going where no shaman's gone before, he accepts his Mission: he shall make us witnesses—though stunned, dumb and deafened we shall, shall be witnesses—of the theomorphic unmasking of Nature.

In a state of enchantment and intent on enchanting others, the narrative psyche performs the unmasking and deposes the false queen, fancying itself, along the way, "allured by the perfidious silences," fancying even silence as possessed by a will to deceive. For this psyche to see "the silent ship" as "manned by sailors in wax," and the waves themselves as "demoniac," is but the taking of enchantment to its logical end: the gradual, inexorable discarding of all that is recognizably human from the story (202).

The discarding itself is horrific and thrilling. Ishmael's refusal to feel his horror helps to explain various anomalous moments in the psychological trajectory of the book.

Why, for instance, does the ragged clothing of the sailors on the first ship the *Pequod* meets look to him like animal skins? Why does he fail to notice, or show no sign of noticing, how macabre his image is?

Why isn't he perturbed?

Doesn't he ever wonder why he sees the way he does? If he does notice, or wonder, why does he toss off the image so blithely, as though, to him, there's nothing surprising in it?

Why isn't there?

Why doesn't it make his skin crawl? Now, at least, in hindsight? Why is there no sign that he gets even one goosebump when,
writing about what happened when he sailed with Captain Ahab,
he remembers how the strange, starving sailors, though passing so
near the *Pequod* that they could leap onto its mast-head, didn't
speak a word, as though, by its mere proximity, they too, even
after all they'd been through, were struck dumb and passive?

Why, when the narrator lets Ahab observe that even shoals of
fish ("small harmless" ones, not their "guilty" cousins) take off in
the opposite direction as soon as they get wind that the *Pequod*'s
coming, sensing it's a vessel with the touch of death—why is his
paramount solicitation to readers not fear for himself and the crew,
or even pity for Ahab, but excitement (203)? He has Ahab mur-
mur, "Swim away from me, do ye?" and says the tone of his voice
reveals more helpless sadness than he's ever shown before.
Promptly, however, he has Ahab turn and thunder at the steersman
"Up helm!" and Ishmael's subsequent Ecclesiastical musings aside,
it is Ahab's customary bark, which to the narrator's ears sounds
like an "old lion's" roar, Ahab's scorning the feeling of sadness that
rose within him, and the narrator's fearful but admiring thrill at his
scorn, that govern the passage (203-4).

At no point does Ahab's bark or his cruelty fail to thrill the
narrator, who routinely hides the cruelty in masking metaphors. In
sentimental masking metaphor he portrays Starbuck's capitulation
to Ahab as a deepening of Starbuck's spirit:

> Oh, life! 'tis in an hour like this, with soul beat down and
> held to knowledge,—as wild, untutored things are forced to
> feed—Oh, life! 'tis now that I do feel the latent horror in thee!
> (148)

In a famous exclamation, in sentimental masking metaphors that
"lift" the debased, mesmerized crew "to the exalted mounts,"
Ishmael prettily endows their debasement with "high qualities,
though dark," with "etherial light," in fact, with a "rainbow"
which, once "spread" over his tale, effectually conceals the disen-
genuous character of the telling (104-5). In the unseeing eyes of the
narrator, dazzled by hardness, Ahab standing motionless, oblivi-
ous, while Captain Gardiner pleads for help to find his son, is a
brave "anvil, receiving every shock, but without the least quivering of his own" (435). Incredibly, he solicits pity not for Captain
Gardiner, who has lost his child, but for Ahab. It is his tone of

voice in such passages which suggests how the author intends us to see—that is, to not see—what the narrator purports to be describing.

For Ishmael, the anvil not quivering represents heroism. Captain Gardiner's supplication is, in his eyes, a blow, and Ahab a Stoic endurer of blows. Such metaphorical conversions signify the oratorical gesture by which the narrator converts Ahab's harsh stubbornness into tragic indomitability. The conversion is not entirely easy, for Ishmael, although he suppresses it, is also sickened by Ahab's arrant lack of compassion. But, like a child in shock, instead of feeling the cruelty, he is dizzied by it. Dizzied, he transports himself into a poetic daze where, obscuring it in metaphor, he makes it unrecognizeable to himself.

By making the obvious unrecognizeable the narrator rationalizes and aggrandises his own submissiveness. He submits and aggrandises because imaginative submission to Ahab is how he imaginatively fuses with him and is, incidentally, empowered to write his book, the vehicle of his, Ahab's and Melville's revenge. Before the unseeing, adoring eyes of narrator and crew, Ahab turns into the collective fantasy: Vanquisher of the White Whale, who lives in his eyes not as life but fire, like the gold doubloon minted in a country in the middle of the world. In the symbolic middle of the ship that is their world, this fantasy is there for all to gaze at and long for, undifferentiated: "I look, you look, he looks; we look, ye look, they look" (362).

What are they looking at?

At Ahab's fantasy, which is winning them over and making them not merely go with him but go "brave" as "fearless fire," fearless since it is "mechanical" (459).

Which suggests that the reader Melville wants is one who, like himself, prefers not to see his story clearly, but instead to become seduced by and in collusion with the metaphors in which he tells it.

Ishmael's own needs as a narrator, needs Melville has given him and shares with him, manifest as the limits of his imagination, an imagination in an unchanging state of shock, and ruled by fear. Were he not, still, even at the end of the book, paralyzed by fear, he might, in reflection at least, see his story differently. He might wonder why everything he looks at looks back at him enchanted. He might even—it's possible!—wonder why, although the scene with Captain Gardiner, also "transfixed" until he starts "from his enchantment," transpires in full view of the crews of both ships, he, the narrator, riveted to Ahab and at pains to convey precisely the quality of Ahab's refusal, delivered "in a voice that prolongingly moulded every word," does not speak of nor appear to see a single man react to Ahab, even furtively, even momentarily, with disgust (435).

The narrator could not and still cannot afford to feel or observe anyone else feeling disgust, or fury since to feel fury would be to render possible not a rhetorical but a genuine striking through the mask of fantasy in which he hides his story from readers and from himself. Instead, through masking metaphors, by the agency of which he obfuscates what is happening, he converts Captain Gardiner's agony to the *Rachel*'s poetic "weeping," and converts terror, loss and death to innocuous pastoral pictures. By the end of the book, then, it will seem scarcely surprising that the *Rachel*'s masts are, for the narrator, "three tall cherry trees," and the men laboring to find a fellow sailor lost on the ocean "boys...cherrying among the boughs" (436).

The cherrying simile is an example of images which, appealing in themselves, are rendered by their context incongruous, if not vicious, and the incongruity does not go away by proposing that Ishmael is being ironic, as is so often proposed in regard to unseasonable imagery in *Moby-Dick*, since the context has no hint of irony about it. What the simile suggests is the extent of the narrator's abstraction from his feelings, the condition of arrested horror in which he remains from the first to the last page of the novel, a horror he has domesticated and grown used to, about which he jokes and puns, a horror as unchanging, habitual and unfelt by him as Ahab's state of misery is habitual and essentially unfelt by him.

Ahab's refusal to help search for his fellow captain's son is inhuman. It is horror, the direct, unmediated impact of Ahab's inhumanity that transfixes Captain Gardiner, causing him, as Ishmael says, to fall more than step back into his boat. Ishmael sees all this, and in some manner empathizes, because Ishmael too is horrified, but rather than feel his horror he converts it to symbiotic thrill.

His thrill feeds the one of the important mysteries he devises: what is Ahab—like an anvil, iron rail, cog, and pyramid—made of?[16] Ishmael's fascination with the body of the whale, his verbal penetration and dissection of it, signifies a displacement of his desire to find out—to not find out—what Ahab is made of. He does not really want to know. Therefore the imagery of trance and seduction proliferates, in a state of suspended nightmare, where nothing seems entirely real. Rather than find out what Ahab is made of, the narrator prefers to see enchantment in every entity that has to do with him, repeatedly invoking the "enchanted air" around and aboard the *Pequod*, the "spell of sleep," the "trance of the sea," the "charmed, churned circle of the hunted sperm whale," the "enchanter's wand" (443, 241, 193).

With each reiteration, and the spreading of the charm across the seascape, the presentiment of retribution that all will share intensifies. Passing into the whale hunt, and into the whales themselves, enchantment puts on, takes off, and puts on again, for the narrator, its face of pain. A whale group appears to him as a "becharmed panic," the fear of the hunted whale appears "chained up and enchanted within him;" harpooned, bleeding whales cannot even die but must die in an agonized "trance" (245, 298, 325). Vengeance spreads over the face of the deep, in a mesmeric glance that overpowers all it touches, and why?

Because the nature of Melville's power as a writer resembles the charismatic species of power possessed by his demon hero, Ahab. This is the charisma of the Ugly Narcissus, which Narcissus becomes the moment his fantasy is over that the face he sees in the water belongs to someone else, for this is the moment when, knowing fully that it is his own image, his desire to possess that image finally and irrevocably vanquishes his desire to love.[17] The gaze makes him "magnetic" precisely because it is inhuman, hearkens backward, inclines to the predatory and, finally, to the bestial. It is the gaze, at one remove, of Ishmael, at two removes, of Melville, refusing to see as other what he seems to look upon, and looking not outward at the world, but inward, at the world as a stepmother by whom he is mesmerized, in hate and desire, a gaze that intends not to see, but to fuse with and expunge.

The author's desire to mesmerize and thereby expunge readers is what gives the characters of *Moby-Dick*, and the narrative sensibility that portrays them, a marionette-like quality. It is why Ishmael's perception is less than autonomous and less than alive, and why he perceives his shipmates as playthings, "painted sailors in wax," or frozen, "like the standing, or stepping, or running skeletons in Herculaneum" (202, 416). It is Melville, himself arrested, who has Ahab conceive himself arrested in eternity as an

Adamic White Whale: "I feel deadly faint, bowed and humped, as though I were Adam, staggering beneath the piled centuries since Paradise" (444), and Melville who has his narrator frighten himself with an Adam eternally, hopelessly longing to die.

The pathos of the narcissistic figure is that, finding himself unbearable, he is not quite sure if he is really alive. His perverseness is that he cultivates his uncertainty.[18]

Cultivating his uncertainty—Am I sure I'm alive? If I am alive, am I me or not me? Do I belong to myself? and if I don't, whose am I and how much?—he agonizes over the possibility that everything else may be as uncertain, and as disingenuous, as he is. In cherished paranoia, he wonders whether the living and nonliving dimensions themselves may not maliciously interpenetrate, and pass for, each other.

The narrator's anxiety on this matter surfaces in his comic discomfiture with the Ramadan, during which Queequeg, reproducing in his posture the "carved image" he worships, exhibits "scarce a sign of active life," and in his terrified fascination with the rumors of knockings in the tombs, with life that is not alive, and death, or non-life, that is (80). Ishmael's fear that what seems to be alive may only be a dead thing playing a trick pervades much of what he sees, from the fossil whale, with "artificial smoke ascending from where the real jet had issued," to Ahab's awareness of sensation in his missing leg, to Blacksmith Perth, left "standing, till the hideous rot of life should make him easier to harvest," to the voracious sharks devouring themselves, to the squid, apparently without sensation, an "unearthly, formless, chance-like apparition of life," which, like Moby-Dick, has no face or front, to the gradual petrification that begins in and spreads outward from Ahab, an "iron statue," with a "stone-carved coat and hat" (375, 401, 237, 400, 438). Such images not only represent the Life that folds Death and the Death that trellises Life, about which the narrator sentimentally muses. They also hint, more bizarrely, of a life than cannot be born existing in a mutually-repellent embrace with a non-life that will not end and cannot die.

Moby-Dick, the apparition of nonlife that cannot die, offers crew and readers a secret object favorably disposed to symbiosis. The psychological content of the secret is buried feeling. In exchange for burying our feelings, we are offered trance, and a realm where autonomy dissolves and identic distinctions—including the distinction between who is speaking and who is listening,

or writer and reader—are blurred. By cajoling us not to differenti-
ate ourselves from the narrator, to obey, and, by obeying, learn to
regard ourselves not as responsive organisms—readers—but as
objects of possession and extensions of himself, Melville invites
readers to become, with him, sublime. If we will see with his eyes,
and disbelieve our own, we won't be sorry, for, in promising to lift
us out of ourselves, he offers participation in the mystical power
that comes from not feeling and not being guilty or afraid of not
feeling.

As Ishmael looks to Ahab and sees in him a vitality which, by
speaking of it ritually, in a spell, the narrator hopes to appropriate,
and Ahab looks to and sees in his White Whale a vitality which,
having maimed him, can alone reverse its spell and make him
whole, so readers too are urged by every possible rhetorical means
to fuse with the narrator, and thus be brought not to life but to that
simulated form of life, Follow Your Leader, which Melville shows
in its rawest form in *Benito Cereno*.

What this means is that Melville's delivery is massive and volcanic precisely because the emotion behind it is maudlin, thwarted
and choked. It means that style swamps content: that style, grand,
aggrandises content into appearing other and more than it is.

It also means that the writer of fiction can dissemble about his
own story. But how can fiction, which does not purport to be phe-
nomenologically "true" in the first place, "lie?"

While the fiction writer does not purport to describe true
events, he is bound, say Hawthorne and James after him, and this
constitutes a tacit understanding between author and reader,
bound to be truthful about the human heart. Though the parameters of such a formulation are as indefinite as one might care to
make them, they are in one respect plain and clear. This is the
respect in which we can say with perfect security that with truth,
as with all earthly matters, part is less than whole.

The lie of *Moby-Dick* is that its truth is partial, and inflated by
the magnifying power of the author's voice to look like whole.
Melville inflates his voice and keeps his eyes fixed on the reader's
to undo the reader and put to sleep the reader's fear of reversion
to savagery, just as Ahab undoes and puts to sleep the humanity of
the *Pequod* crew.

Piloted by one who fantasizes that his "tiller was, somehow, in
some enchanted way, inverted," the readers *Moby-Dick* seeks and
presupposes can be brought to such a degree of excitement by col-

lective hate that they will regress, will go backwards into a condition of being antecedent to autonomous selfhood and in significant ways to humanness itself (354). In this condition readers' eyes meets author's "as the bloodshot eyes of prairie wolves meet the eyes of their leader," a leader who scorns to distinguish self from other or death from life, and takes pride in his scorn (145).

Notes

1. Daniel Wilson, "Readers in Texts" in *PMLA* 96, 1981, pp. 848-863, and Wolfgang Iser, *The Act of Reading*, pp. 126-155.

2. The reader whom the writer unconsciously fantasizes and invokes, ninety-nine parts mystery, may be one part "narcissistic libido [that] has never really turned outward," writes Weiskel in regard to Shelley's "Alastor" (*The Romantic Sublime*, p. 146). Libido that cannot, because it is blocked and forbidden, turn outward, is the genesis of what Alice Miller calls "the concealed tragedy of childhood:" the repetition compulsion, whereby the child of a narcissistically disturbed parent becomes spellbound to the parent and develops the disturbance himself, the "many and varied enactments" of which "are essentially a crying out for understanding..." (*Good*, pp. 66, 180, 241-242).

3. In the opening pages of *Our Adult World* Melanie Klein proposes that unconscious fantasy is akin to a neurological function:

> As my friend the late Susan Isaacs put it in her paper on this subject..."Phantasy is...the mental corollary, the psychic representative of instinct. There is no impulse...which is not experienced as unconscious phantasy..." (p.6).

Freud, for whom "the unconscious" is often metaphorical, suggests that it fantasizes constantly, subsists in a state of fantasy, and shapes not simply particular wishes and fears but the emotional landscape in which imaginative activity occurs—a concept pertinent to the "deep text" of literary theory.

4. Regarding the way Ahab looks at the crew, Blau writes: "Not only is Ahab's attention fixated, but his gaze has become a blind stare...Ahab is a somnambulist entranced in his nightmare of power" (*The Body Impolitic*, p. 105).

What I am describing as the way Melville "looks" at readers resembles Alice Miller's allusions to "those things we cannot see through...that we have absorbed through our mother's eyes—eyes and an attitude from which no reading or learning can free us." Miller is discussing envy, and how a narcissistic mother "trains her child with looks:"

In her own baby, such a mother sees the split-off and never-experienced part of her self, of whose breakthrough into consciousness she is afraid, and whom she...now envies (*Drama*, pp. 86, 100).

5.   In *The Four Fundamental Concepts of Psychoanalysis*, Lacan speaks at length about "the gaze." Especially pertinent to the present study is "The Split between the Eye and the Gaze," pp. 67-79, Lacan's discussion of loneliness in "The Subject and the Other: Alienation" pp. 203-216, and his comments regarding "the gaze" in Sartre's *Being and Nothingness*.

Stern speaks of the "essential friendlessness in Melville's works" ("Melville, Society and Language," *A Companion*, 466). Martin discusses Melville's abiding sense of isolation, calling him an "extraordinarily lonely man... almost all of whose books depict the search for friendship." He suggests that Ilbrahim, the protagonist of Hawthorne's wrenching story "The Gentle Boy," may be a precursor to Ishmael, and that his death, and the death of the faun in *The Marble Faun*, represents Hawthorne's vision of the fate of male friendship, as well as "a psychological portrait of the eventual suppression of the androgynous" (*Hero, Captain, and Stranger*, pp. 94-97). Higgins and Parker suggest that as Melville started Pierre, he was "Overwhelmed by his affinity for Hawthorne...to the point of wanting to write only for him..." ("Reading *Pierre*," *A Companion*, p. 221).

6.   In the novel this dynamic is explicit in the relationship of Ahab to Fedallah. More often, scholars consider Fedallah (or the White Whale) a type of *doppelganger* to Ahab:

Ahab and his intended prey are doubles. Both have ribbed brows, wry mouths, and withered   or stricken limbs. Both share an apparent spirit of conscious malice...(*Twentieth-Century Interpretations of* Moby-Dick, p. 40.)

Cameron also addresses the *doppelganger*:

Of course, doubles and complementarities, like identic instabilities, exist in all fiction. Yet in Eurcpean fiction... characters inhabited by others are generally haunted by them. They feel terror rather than pleasure at the otherness in their midst. In *Moby-Dick*, on the other hand, Ahab experiences his internalized counterpart, Fedallah, with neither pleasure nor horror. He seems undisturbed by the question of Fedallah's relation to him, unconfused by the man Melville means us to see as problematically at once inside and outside of him (*Corporeal Self*, p. 541).

7.   Ishmael says the White Whale's face is unlocateable: a dangerous, dreamy secret. The face of Hawthorne, imaginatively superimposed

upon that of Maria Gansevoort, may illuminate ambiguities to which I
previously alluded regarding the White Whale's gender. "He is a he, with
the body that Ahab and Ishmael long for," writes Leverenz. "Yet he is also
nonhuman, feline and devouring, always surrounded with cream and
milkiness that can never be touched..."

> The often-described "high, pyramidal white hump" of Moby
> Dick, his most striking feature, clearly associates these origins
> with the breast, but always in that context of untouchable
> strangeness (*Moby-Dick*, in *Psychoanalysis and Literary
> Process*, pp. 103, 104).

8.   Edgar Dryden, discussing enchantment and "transfusion,"
makes a similar point with respect to Hawthorne: "Hawthorne's characters seem especially threatened by any relationship that implies the 'transfusion of one spirit into another...'" (LL 1, 62)

> For Hawthorne the act of reading is a compelling, mysterious,
> perhaps even dangerous occupation. Writers, after all, possess
> strange powers of enchantment that allow them to cast hyp-
> notic spells over their readers...as Holgrave does to Phoebe
> when he reads her his story of Alice Pyncheon. His words are
> like a 'veil' that by enveloping her insures that she will
> "behold only him, and live only in his thoughts and emo-
> tions" (CE II, 211)...For Hawthorne the fascination of read-
> ing, like the fascination of love, is the result of the irresistible
> lure exerted by   another person's existence, but, unlike the
> relation between the beloved and the lover, that between
> author and reader is generated by a will to power...(*Poetics*,
> 111, 107).

Charvat suggests that Melville was in a "conflict with his readers, which
lasted the whole ten years of his professional writing life" (*The Profession
of Authorship*, p. 204)
9.   The eerily unchanging, frozen quality of the hunt for the White
Whale, and its overlay of furious activity, constitute both its curse and spe-
cialness. What Richard Chase says regarding The Encantadas applies to
Moby-Dick:

> The special curse which "exalts" the islands "in desolation"
> is that they never change; they know neither autumn nor
> spring; they are transfixed in a seasonless waste. Yet there is
> the continual illusion of change, of pantomimic, protean
> movement (Chase's *Herman Melville*, p. 211).

Blau observes,

> Whatever the years that have intervened, Ishmael remains
> what he was. He still goes "sailing about a little"...Ishmael's
> only hope for escape lies in his ability to maintain a state of
> constant movement (*The Body Impolitic*, p. 59).

Kinney discusses the lack of change in the protagonist, Clarel, in Melville's
poem, and the absence of "the possibility of change" (*"Clarel,"* A
Companion, p. 402). Tolchin notices in Melville's early work the association of coldness and stillness with castration. In *Typee*, he writes, "it is
precisely the death-like coldness that threatens to unman Tommo by inca-
pacitating his leg" (*Mourning*, p. 38).

    10.   Melville's purported declaration that his mother hated him, first
referred to by Weaver, may be the single most frequently cited statement
of later biographers, some of whom dispute whether Melville actually
made it:

> Of his mother he is reported to have said in later life: "She
> hated me." It seems not altogether fantastic to contend that
> the Gorgon face that Melville bore in his heart; the goading
> impalpable image that made his whole life a pilgrimage of
> despair: that was the cold beautiful face of his mother, Maria
> Gansevoort.

Weaver also cites, from *Pierre*: "The face!—the face!—The face steals
down upon me" (*Mariner and Mystic*, pp. 62, 66).

    Tolchin probes Weaver's Gorgon image. His first chapter efficiently sum-
marizes scholarship concerning Melville's relationship with his mother,
which Murray sees as perenially shadowed by Maria's "prohibiting dis-
positions" ("In Nomine Diaboli" in *Critical Essays on Herman Melville's
Moby-Dick*, ed. Higgins and Parker, pp. 408-420).

    11.   In *Depression and the Body*, in a chapter entitled "Horror: The
Face of Unreality," Lowen writes that the intrigue stems from early trau-
ma which the organism wards off, and, at the same time, investigates—
voyeuristically, as though it happened to someone else—by magical thinking. The extent to which the characters in *Moby-Dick* sound as though
they are collectively sleepwalking as they meekly follow the chief sleepwalker, Ahab, may represent how much Melville abstracted himself from
his own feelings. In this regard I was interested to learn that Hitler is
recorded as having said, shortly after the conquest of the Rhineland, "I
follow my course with the security and precision of a sleepwalker"
("Seduction of a Nation," BBC television documentary aired in New York
in November, 1991).

    12.   Such enemies, according to Klein, are born in the "unconscious
fantasy of feeling deprived and persecuted by the breast which refuses to
give...satisfaction." The local "real" enemy is thus transfigured into an
ubiquitous potential enemy, who may materialize anywhere, in the form

of anyone who promises to fulfill the original craving for love. The very
fact of the promise awakens the suspicion that the promiser will renege,
which is why (s)he—I am speaking of crew and readers—must be watched
with such a "heedful, closely calculating attention" (*Our Adult World*, pp.
2-5, 18).

13.   Wolf and Weiskel discuss Gothic features of punishment in their
studies of romantic fiction. Ahab's stratagem psychically to beat Starbuck
down is Gothic to the core; Starbuck calls it being "overmanned," and
says that Ahab "drilled deep down...the ineffable thing has tied me to him;
tows me with a cable I have no knife to cut" (*Moby-Dick*, p. 148). What
is this uncuttable "cable" that ties, tows, punishes with love and belongs
to a "he" who's a "she" and is also, as Leverenz writes, nonhuman? What
is this "lurid woe would shrivel me up" (*Moby-Dick*, p. 148)? The
Punitive Umbilicus. Miller could be interpreting Ahab's—Ishmael's?—fear
of mutiny—and birth—when she describes

> the fear of a possible resurrection and return of the split-off
> parts of the self. This is why beating is a never-ending task—
> behind it hovers fear of the emergence of one's own repressed
> weakness, humiliation, and helplessness, which one has tried
> to escape all one's life by means of grandiose behavior (*Good*,
> p. 188).

Rogin also senses the potent, confused significance of punishment for
Melville, although he does not suggest, as I do, that it is central to in
Melville's vision of his readers:

> Melville's early fiction repudiated the whip. But there were
> also signs of a forbidden attraction to it, suggesting that at the
> same time it punished disobedience and desire, it was as well
> a sign of love (*Subversive Genealogies*, p. 189).

14.   Edinger cites James Kirsch regarding the "self-estrangement of
the ruled," their habit, willingness, and eagerness to feel like strangers to
themselves. Kirsch looks at how the narcissistic subsuming of other
aspects of the personality in the will

> produces a remarkable increase of the intellect and of power
> over other human beings but which is dehumanizing. Thus
> demonized, the ego subjects individuals and groups to its own
> wishes and goals, assimilates them into its own system and
> estranges them from themselves morally and in every other
> way. Such a *Gottahnlichkeit* ultimately leads to the destruc-
> tion...of all who willingly accept this power (*Melville's* Moby-
> Dick: *A Jungian Commentary*, p. 66).

15.   In "Seduction of a Nation," it is suggested that not only did Dr.
Goebbels develop his mastery of the techniques of propaganda by studying American advertising, but, with perverse reciprocity worthy of the

most scathing Swiftian satire, American advertising firms have continued to learn from Goebbels. A Mr. Harvey Thomas, International Public Relations Consultant, has this to say while viewing film clips of rallies in Berlin in 1933, "rallies which," says the documentary narrator, "modern media organizers now regard with awe:"

> Watching Hitler being brought in through the crowd was quite interesting because we're only just now beginning in political and commercial terms to use the same kind of pre-sentational techniques that Hitler was using forty or fifty years ago...He knows exactly the mood of his audience, which means he's studied it very carefully. He's actually obeying the basic principles:...knowing your audience, knowing what they're looking for, knowing what you want them to do.

The documentary details how Hitler "offered ritual, the thrill of immersion in a vast pagan rite which still had the familiar overtones of religious practice." A Mr. Egon Hanfstaengl, identified as "son of an early Nazi supporter," remembers "the animal contact" at the rallies, which, he says, loosened inhibitions so that the audience became, as it were, one person, and reverted to behaviors which, as individuals, would nauseate them.

16.   For Cameron, "the repetitive and feverish question of *Moby-Dick* [is]: of what are bodies made?" (*The Corporeal Self*, p. 4.)

17.   I am borrowing Zoellner's fruitful concept, although arguing for a reading of *Moby-Dick* which differs fundamentally from that put forth in *The Salt-Sea Mastadon*. Zoellner's work, despite the questions it raises about Melville's novel, is part of the critical tradition that sees Ishmael as an innocent narrator and Ahab an object-lesson (pp. 94, 100-103, 115, 117).

18.   Chase, citing Lawrence, discusses the "horror of reversion, of undoing" in Melville's work (Chase's *Herman Melville*, p. 15). Julia Kristeva suggests that The horror! the horror! is not just horrible but possesses compelling powers of attraction: Conrad's "fascination of the abomination." William H. Shurr's *The Mystery of Iniquity: Melville as Poet, 1857-1891* examines some of the same issues.

Kazin makes a related point: "...there is in Melville a cold, final, ferocious hopelessness, a kind of ecstatic masochism, that delights in punishing...man, in heaping coals on his head, in drowning him" (*American Critical Essays*, p. 46).

Of ecstatic masochism, the mother, horror, hopelessness, homosexuality, the White Whale and my suggestions in this chapter about how Melville imagines his readers, I refer once more to Alice Miller. She is citing the German writer, Erika Burkart:

Whoever inquires about our childhood wants to know something about our soul. If the question is not just a rhetorical
one and the questioner has the patience to listen, he will come
to realize that we love with horror and hate with an inexpli-
cable love whatever caused us our greatest pain and difficul-
ty. (*Good*, p. 3)

Chapter 4

Fusion

Fusion occurs when a figure in authority imbues those subject to his authority with the delusion that he is them and they are him.

The intensity of Melville's fusion with readers derives from his success in conflating oratory, the object of which is persuasion, with poetry, which does not have an object.

Peggy Noonan's "Thousand Points of Light" trope in the 1988 acceptance speech she wrote for George Bush at the G.O.P. national convention is an example of such conflation, whose practitioners are by no means limited to demagogues, Republicans or politicians. Fusion requires repetition, espouses altruistic goals and is a skill of master rhetoricians. Melville's genius in *Moby-Dick* is how his 1851 novel anticipates increasingly sophisticated techniques of linguistic fusion in the twentieth century, by which an author(ity) implies and successfully persuades mass audiences that the story they are hearing, though they may not know or want to know it, they themselves wrote.

But aren't all good authors seductive and don't all fuse with readers, insofar as they succeed in drawing readers into the universe of the story, even to the extent of making us feel, as James says, that we have lived another life?

Yes. What makes the seductiveness of *Moby-Dick* exceptionally potent is that it stems not from the author's successfully transporting readers to the decks of the *Pequod*, but from his manner of convincing us to be secret, chosen, special sharers.[1] It is this sense of the author in intimate, unholy collusion with readers, a collusion so sensitive that the narrator becomes what Jung calls the "shadow" self, that creates the peculiar and extraordinary undercurrent of ventriloquism in *Moby-Dick*, and the sense that Ishmael is telling his story not as though it happened to him, but to us.[2]

What happens to us is prefigured in the image to which I alluded at the close of the last chapter, when "the bloodshot eyes of the prairie wolves meet the eyes of their leader." This image, depicting the crew surrendering all sense of boundary between themselves and Ahab, is the heart of the novel. They are intoxicated, according to Ishmael, by the sight of the gold doubloon and by the potion, "hot as Satan's hoof" (145), Ahab passes round. These acts, however, are but the ceremonial accoutrements of what intoxicates them most: surrender itself, surrender to Ahab's talk, which invests the ceremony with an aura of grandeur and thereby masks what they and he are doing. Unmasked, that is to say, freed from the narrator's narcissistic spin, what we glimpse in starkest terms in "The Quarter-Deck" scene is the gathering devolutionary momentum that shapes the tale—the momentum evinced also when Ishmael wakes at the tiller and imagines the *Pequod* rushing backwards—and carries it to its end. When, moreover, Ishmael imagines Ahab as a wolf and the crew as his wolf pack we also glimpse the quite specific relation to the author into which we as readers are drawn.

This relation is that of a tempter to his subject. But the fall to temptation that the *Pequod* crew enacts as they let themselves be taken over serves only as the beginning of an analysis of what happens to readers. I say "temptation" rather than "damnation," for although Ahab dares and taunts, teases and goads his men to hunt the White Whale and be damned, it is not, immediately at least, hell, or, if it is hell, it is a particular room, the waiting room, to which Melville invites readers.

The waiting room of hell, which Melville enters and does not leave, is where it is revealed to him that he does not belong on earth, in "this visible world" (169). The waiting room of hell is where he learns that the living in which his body, where he does not belong either, involves him, is a trap, contrived by a thing neither here nor there, male nor female, dead nor alive. The place from whence he beckons, this waiting room, is where he receives his Mission to reveal to humanity that he and we were "formed in fright," and that human dignity requires us to join in a losing battle that should never have been in the first place, which he—we—

should never have had to fight: the unfair, unchanging, causeless, hopeless combat that invests all created nature as it strains to be fed, loved and freed of its punitive maker.

Ishmael is an orphan, he says in the last word of the book, and his adventure at sea the tale of a stepmother world. It is also a scream for a world that would be a mother.[3] In "The Counterpane," the only tender chapter of the novel, this cry appears wonderfully close to the textual surface. Like his discourse on nursing whales in "The Grand Armada," with its "enchanted pond" where whale babies, "while yet drawing mortal nourishment," seem to be "still spiritually feasting upon some unearthly reminiscence," like "A Squeeze of the Hand" where he fuses with shipmates and readers—"Come...let us squeeze ourselves into each other; let us squeeze ourselves into the very milk and sperm of kindness"—it is the narrator's coded cry for love (325, 349).

The love he longs for is that of the earliest stage of life, characterized by the infant's fusion with the mother.

The chapter begins as Ishmael opens his eyes and sees as "blended" and inseparable the colors of the quilt that keeps him warm and Queequeg's tatooed, protective, loving arm:

> Indeed, partly lying on it as the arm did when I first awoke, I could hardly tell it from the quilt, they so blended their hues together; and it was only by the sense of weight and pressure that I could tell that Queequeg was hugging me. (32)

The only scene of voluntary physical intimacy in the book evokes the narrator's only memory, in which dream and reality have blended indistinguishably: "whether it was a reality or a dream, I could never entirely settle" (32). The memory concerns Ishmael and his "stepmother," "who, somehow or other, was all the time whipping me, or sending me to bed supperless" (32).

To punish him for crawling up the chimney, the stepmother makes him go to bed in the middle of the day, the longest day in the year, a circumstance that sharpens his misery. She punishes Ishmael by leaving him alone, after humiliating him by dragging him down from the chimney by his legs. More painful even than this, however, is Ishmael's sense that although she won't let him go, she does not want him, either. He doesn't feel he belongs to his family, and sees himself not as a member of it but a strange and none too welcome guest. His bedroom is the "little room in the third floor" at the top of the house, and he apparently has no ally, since, although he will hear "gay voices all over the house," they, like the stepmother, remain faceless (32-3). Not only does no one come to his aid; they do not seem in the least aware of his misery.

Does anyone even notice he's not there? Ishmael must wonder, likening himself to the "little sweep," an Old World image of a poor, forlorn child left alone in the world to fend for himself (32). The stepmother, meanwhile, is impervious to his plea that she give him "a good slippering" instead of making him stay in bed, and thus begins, says the narrator, a span of hours during which he felt "a great deal worse than I have ever done since, even from the greatest subsequent misfortunes" (33).

He will never forget this day, or the "mystery" of the night that follows, during which he wakes to sense near him a "nameless, unimaginable silent form or phantom" whose "supernatural" hand he holds.[4] Ishmael freezes with terror, but cannot let go of the hand. He will never know, he says, whether it was real. Nor will he ever know, suggest to readers, or even bring to his own consciousness the possibility that the hand he could not release may have been that of the "stepmother—"which might be his angry name for his natural mother—herself.[5]

The only feeling he describes regarding his memory of the night is fear:

> For what seemed ages piled on ages, I lay there, frozen with the most awful fears, not daring to drag away my hand; yet ever thinking that if I could but stir it one single inch, the horrid spell would be broken. (33)

Evidently, though, this is not all he felt, for he continues:

> Now, take away the awful fear, and my sensations at feeling the supernatural hand in mine were very similar, in their strangeness, to those which I experienced on waking up and seeing Queequeg's arm thrown round me. (33)

What are those other sensations, the ones left when we take away the fright?

What Ishmael feels when he wakes in Queequeg's arms is pleasure.[6] Overnight, unconsciously, he has moved close to Queequeg, just as overnight, unconsciously, he came into physical contact with the supernatural figure. The first experience terrified him, he says; the other made him feel safe. In both Ishmael is entirely passive. His passivity, and the strange feeling of falling asleep alone and waking up near someone else, someone physically powerful, who is or is like a stranger, and has threatened him earlier, is his conscious link between the two situations. The unconscious link is Melville's fantasy of turning the punishing, uncontrollable stepmother into a good, protective mother. This scene, along with Ishmael's experiences at and leading up to the inn called "Peter Coffin," also represents the author's fantasy of reconfiguring and controlling readers.

He will control us by teaching us how to come to a more authentic birth, in a more authentic universe, the negative universe, in our true status: orphans with a vengeance. He will teach us by example.[7]

Ishmael's pursuit of willed rebirth constitutes the first third of the novel, up to the appearance of Ahab, whose own pursuit supplants it. Dying to the visible world that was "formed in love," a love he never got, the narrator will come to a new kind of life among the "invisible spheres...formed in fright," where he has always, in any case, been.[8]

He is on his way out of this world, where he never belonged, where he is a lost soul, to a world that came before it. That is why, when he is on land, he is like someone lost at sea. It is why, in the character of an unloved stranger in a strange, cold, dark place, he leaves what appears to be his original home, "the good city of *Old* Manhatto," for a temporary new one, *New* Bedford (my italics), a type of way-station where he "duly arrive[s]" (17). What duly arrives is Ishmael's soul, for which New Bedford represents the port of embarkation. In the narrator's re-birth in vengeance, by which he will rid himself of the hypos that made him want to die, lies the coded expression of his search for a mother to bear him, and his, and Melville's, experience of the womb.

The first womb, Maria Gansevoort Melville's, a mother often regarded as a stepmother by her second son, was wrong, and delivered him, perhaps with conscious malice, to the wrong world.[9] The womb through which Ishmael will find his way past the fraudulent visible to the true invisible planets will be right. It must not be excessively female, this womb, but not "mannish," like Maria Gansevoort Melville, either. Above all it must not be too alive. If he is lucky it will benevolently ignore his presence within it.

Passing by the "too expensive and too jolly" Crossed Harpoons, and the "bright red windows" of the Sword-Fish Inn, from which pour, along with "such fervent rays" that they seem to melt packed snow and ice, phallic implications that scare him so much he does not even approach, Ishmael, who can scarcely see where he is or where he is going, pauses for the first time at a building with two doors, an outer one which is open and an inner one which is closed: "I came to a smoky light proceeding from a low, wide building, the door of which stood invitingly open" (18).

There are vaginal suggestions to this structure, as contrasted to the two previous ones. Vaguely it reminds him of—what else?—a prostitute: "It had a careless look, as if it were meant for the uses of the public" (18). Ishmael enters—and immediately falls down, stumbling against an ash-box whose contents, the first and one of the few items our narrator ever has in his mouth, almost choke him. In another image which, like that of antique Adam, suggests that no time has elapsed between the first book of the Old Testament and the setting of *Moby-Dick*, Ishmael wonders if the ashes he is tasting come from "that destroyed city, Gomorrah" (18).

Why does Ishmael have Gomorrah on his mind? Why is this place, which may be Gomorrah, also "The Trap" (18)? He doesn't say, but, curious, "pushes" on, and opens the inner door. He then discovers what looks to him like a Parliament in Hell—which prompts him to "back out" and "move on." His movement through the still, frigid town has a quality of floating. It continues until he reaches a sign painted with "a tall straight jet of misty spray..." The inn to which the sign is attached, while phallic in name, is not threateningly so since it appears, on the outside at least, "quiet," "dilapidated," one side (like the she-world, Nature) "palsied," the entrance reminding him of a "condemned old craft" (18-19).[10]

The narrator, like readers, ever "moving on," finds his way from one inn to another, each with a kind of fatality seeming to point to the next, until he arrives at the one that tells in its name the complicated story he is about to enact, the-spouter-in-Peter-Coffin.

The Spouter-Inn, nominally male, like Ishmael, though possessing a "wide, low, straggling entry," resembles him in a number of other ways too, not least in that it is not what it appears to be (20). Its outside, posing little obvious menace, gives little clue to its inside, teeming with images of darkness, ancient pain and death. Ishmael immediately recognizes it as just what he is looking for.

He is right, of course: the Spouter Inn will present him, at last, with Queequeg. On the way to Queequeg, he tells readers what we feel on beholding the Inn's interior. They are feelings of horror,

Ishmael's early childhood feelings—"those first feelings," writes
Emily Bronte, in another vein, "that were born with me"—and
recapitulate those of the young boy immobilized in the "horrid
spell" (33). From all sides, first from the painting "that fairly froze
you to it," then from the opposite wall—"You shuddered as you
gazed"—as it is "hung all over with a heathenish array of mon-
strous clubs and spears," and, mixed among them, "rusty old
whaling lances and harpoons all broken and deformed," the Inn
announces itself as the birthing stage of a journey backward (20-
1).

The atavistic character of this journey, towards the prehuman,
may account for the confusion of phallic and vaginal imagery
abounding in "The Spouter-Inn" and "The Counterpane" chapters. Ishmael, worrying about the need to "sleep in your own
skin," is about to be reborn (24).

His new mother, like his old one, may be strange, but the
strangeness will be endurable since the new mother will be male.
An ideal replacement mother, he will possess virtues dramatically
lacking in his predecessor. He will rarely speak, never complain,
never chide, live by his harpoon, which he wields cautiously and
with consummate skill, and will be, besides, simple and affectionate. By sleeping next to this phallic mother—"a creature," not
unlike Ishmael, "in the transition stage"—Ishmael may even be
changed into a kind of girl-child, or, at least, a neuter, which suggests that in the narrator's comic presentation of himself as
Queequeg's nervous virgin bride is a sense of adulthood, as well as
manhood, happily waived (34).

Queequeg will be the inverse of the stepmother, and that is
why Ishmael's transfiguring midwinter night with him, during
which, he says, "I...never slept better in my life," calls up the mid-
summer night of terror during which, "for ages piled on ages," he,
like Adam, also brought down from bliss by woman, lay in
accursed wakefulness. His first room was "little;" this one is
"small." Both are upstairs, in a jolly house of strangers among
whom he feels unwanted. In both places he seems to be younger
than the other occupants, a novice who does not know the rules of
the game among veterans who may toy with him to amuse themselves—a possibility about which, in the later episode, he has
learned to be on guard: "you'd better stop spinning that yarn to
me," he says, trying to hold his own against the teasing landlord,
"I'm not green" (26, 32-3).

He is green. This time, though, it will be right. Queequeg will make it so.[11] The inquisitive child who tried to explore the inside of the chimney and got punished will not be punished now, though he reemerges in the curiosity with which Ishmael, less like a bride peering at her husband than a young boy fascinated by his mother, watches Queequeg wash and dress: "I was guilty of great rudeness; staring at him from the bed, and watching all his toilette motions" (34). He will watch with special attention the way Queequeg puts away his weapons, by which act, as though quieting and temporarily disarming himself of his own maleness, Queequeg wins Ishmael's love. Where the stepmother "somehow or other, was all the time whipping or sending me to bed supperless," Queequeg is "kind and charitable," treating Ishmael with such marked "civility and consideration" that even the "hatchet-faced baby" of a tomahawk that "sleeps" between them, instead of frightening him, makes Ishmael feel, for the only time in the story, safe (31, 34).

The narrator is recasting the night when he woke in a room "wrapped in outer darkness" with his arm hanging vulnerably "over the counterpane" and his body frozen in fear (33). That night has become this morning; that counterpane, which did not keep him warm, has become this counterpane, in the folds of which he wakes at daylight with Queequeg's protective arm thrown over him "in the most loving and affectionate manner" (32). Ishmael feels so safe with Queequeg that he will even, for a while, feel his natural appetites, dormant until now and nonexistent for the rest of the book, come to life. The cold, tired traveller who arrived the night before and, in his depressed condition, said nothing about feeling hungry, speaks in the morning, with relish, of breakfast, and of New Bedford as the Promised Land of oil, corn and wine, as well as eggs and milk (38).

Ishmael is loved. He will come to speak of the "strange feelings," the "melting" in him towards Queequeg, the sense of being "mysteriously drawn towards him" as if by "magnets" (53). With the peacefulness a child who is loved feels towards its mother, Ishmael makes Queequeg his "bosom friend," easily, without anxiety, since he "seemed to take to me quite as naturally and unbiddenly as I to him" (53). Queequeg's acceptance, awakening the narrator to his orality, also prompts him to one of the only requests he makes in the novel: "a social smoke" on "that wild pipe" of Queequeg's. Any remaining "ice of indifference...in the

Pagan's breast" thaws, when he offers his pipe, as a nursing mother offers her breast, to his grateful friend. The two settle into a
calm rhythm of understanding, with Queequeg's pipe, now belong-
ing to both, "regularly passing between us," and Queequeg urging
Ishmael to "unite" with him (53-4).

The beatific unity is short-lived.[12] Despite Ishmael's resolution
to stay with Queequeg "like a barnacle," once he sees Ahab, the
relationship fades (61). Ishmael has not been weaned, but he cannot sustain his feelings for Queequeg, either, perhaps because they
remind him too acutely of what never was and will never be. The
new, deadly life to which the narrator is reborn through Queequeg
leads to the vessel, chosen for both by Ishmael, where Queequeg
will drown and Ishmael survive atop his unreadable coffin.

The longing remains, but displaced and abstracted. The lethal,
seductive mother, who never truly left, returns, larger and more
irresistible than ever, and now it is Ahab, in whom the narrator
subsumes himself, who seeks her vengeful suckling. It is not that
Ahab wants to. It is that he can't, according to Ishmael, help it.
The cruel, twisted, heavenly body that sheds "milky" "irresistible
enticings" and even makes the waters white like milk, the body
that leaves a starry, shining "milky-way wake of creamy foam, all
spangled with golden gleamings," and whose "milky whiteness" is
the constant meditation of the tale, draws Ahab—so he proclaims,
angrily—nearer and nearer.

Ahab, in fact, no matter where he is, how near or far away, is
in the White Whale's orbit, precisely as Ishmael, leaving Queequeg,
is in Ahab's. He senses its movements and believes he intuits its
thoughts. The more it eludes him, seeming always just beyond his
reach, the more ardent grows his pursuit, for he is afraid that he is
in its power, and his fear fuses him to it.

Fear, and a desperate desire to prove that he isn't afraid, is the
content of the narrative preoccupation with the size, features and
anatomy of the whale.

Fear, and the need to punish those who, he knows, may not
believe him, is why the narrator seeks to mesmerize his readers.

To mesmerize and take away another's feelings is to penetrate
and make the other disappear, to swallow him whole, and, from
Ishmael's being swallowed up by his own words to the final scene
of the Pacific Ocean swallowing the *Pequod*, *Moby-Dick* is about
wanting to be pierced and devoured, and fighting against the
desire. Ahab is fighting the desire until at last, on the symbolic

third day of his chase, he strangles on it, ignominiously hanged by the very thing that, like a deadly umbilicus, attaches him to Moby-Dick.

Strangulation, asphyxiation, the cutting-off of breath, being eternally, vengefully towed "to pieces, while still chasing thee, though tied to thee" suggest the unnumbered deaths of his soul Melville, behind his Ishmael, behind his Ahab, died (468). If the Albany critic's sense of Melville strangling his own child was correct, moreover, there is a consideration even sadder, which is that Melville did not die deeply enough to permit himself to speak out against the real tragedy: that the whale has the whole ocean in which to move and feel and express himself, but Ahab, Ishmael and Melville do not. Perhaps the most poignant feature of Melville's writing is the sense of how deeply he needed to feel free, as a writer and as a man. Instead of freedom he lived and wrote as though in bondage. That is why the mightiness of voice in *Moby-Dick*, which is the power of the book, resembles the helpless, hopeless rattling of his jail bars by a prisoner, a sound to ward off not just silence, but tears.

Notes

1.   In the winter of 1849, during the most intense period of Melville's friendship with her husband, which coincided with the composition of *Moby-Dick*, Sophia Hawthorne wrote
several letters in which she attempts to describe the younger writer. Edwin Miller, in his moving account of Melville's "strangely intense relationship" with Hawthorne, in which, says Miller, Melville was "a fierce wooer" and "clearly the pursuer" who, as the relationship waned, "forced himself on Hawthorne," discusses these letters at length. He concludes that Sophia Hawthorne, like others who knew Melville, was, at first, "enormously attracted" by his "virile presence" (*Melville*, pp. 41-43, 182, 190, 286-7).
Melville's biographers, Parker especially, frequently celebrate what they see as the virility of his writing, which, like Miller and Parker, they presume to have been qualities of the man himself, qualities those around him felt and responded to. Perhaps Sophia Hawthorne was, as Miller suggests, "perplexed but fascinated" (p. 44). I find the letters, as well as recorded remarks by Sophia Hawthorne about her husband's friend, cryptic. What strikes her most is the expression in Melville's eyes, and it is by no means clear that what she sees there is entirely appealing to her. She speaks of his "dim, indrawn look" and "strange, lazy glance...with a power in it quite unique. It does not seem to penetrate through you but to take you into himself" (p. 44). Much of what I have to say about fusion grew from this observation by Sophia Hawthorne.

2.   Melville's visit to the Shaker settlement and his interest in the Shakers, "well-attested" according to Merton Sealts, Jr., as cited in Dorothee Finkelstein's *Melville's Orienda*, brings to mind a related point regarding what I call his way of "looking" at the reader. According to Sealts, "what seemingly attracted him most was the prophetic strain in the Shaker religion, with its association of exalted bodily and mental states," the type of euphoria that, in my reading of *Moby-Dick*, creates the hypnotic stare through which Ahab fuses with the crew and Melville with readers.

Finkelstein notes that in 1849 Melville obtained from his friend and publisher Bentley a copy of William Beckford's *Vathek*, whose Manfredian protagonist closely resembles Ahab, not least in "his glance...characteristic of the Carlylean hero as Prophet" (*Orienda*. pp. 198, 224). If, as Lawrence Thompson says, Melville falls in love with Ahab, it may be because gazing with Ahab's eyes allows him to revisit the unconscious fantasies of his earliest years—this time, however, not in the role of vulnerable child, but seductive parent.

3.   Melville, the biographers say, adored Hawthorne, and Hawthorne, initially interested, even thrilled, became ambivalent. Chase calls the friendship "abortive," largely because "Hawthorne had been uncomfortable with a sense of the burdensome psychic demands of an imperfect titan whose sex was somewhat ambiguous" (p. 288). Much scholarship explores how Melville may have translated unmet childhood needs to other men, and how the loss of Hawthorne's friendship, from which he seems never to have recovered, manifests in his work. The following citations are glimpses of what is said on the matter: Mumford (pp. 264-5), Chase (pp. 6-9, 113), Haberstroh (pp. 104-7), Howard (pp. 77, 153), Martin (pp. 14-15, 63, 102-3), Eleanor Melville Metcalf (*Cycle*, p. 83), Edwin Miller (pp. 182, 190, 286-7) Barbour (*A Companion*, p. 12), Shurr (*A Companion*, p.364).

Particularly sensitive is Miller's analysis of Julian Hawthorne's memoir recounting his father's elation at the famous picnic with the Duyckincks and Melville on August 5, 1850, after which Hawthorne purportedly told his son that he "loved Mr. Melville" as much as he loved his wife and children, and the later, heartbreaking meeting of the two writers on November 12, 1856 on the sand dunes at Liverpool.

Dillingham says Hawthorne was to Melville an "ideal priest," and concurs with others that "No one before Hawthorne or after ever performed the same function for Melville" (*Later Novels*, p. 126).

4.   Blau discusses "the prerogatives of the vertical:"

> Sleep...is a dangerous time for a man unsure of his relations
> with the world. To prostrate the self is to make it vulnera-
> ble...At such times he [Ishmael] shares with the rest of hunt-
> ed animal life the fear that he will be eaten. Grasped by a
> mysterious hand, he imagines that he is already in what Elias

Canetti calls "the anteroom of the mouth and the stomach"
of his pursuer (*The Body Impolitic*, p. 95).

5.   I am indebted to my colleague Louise Dutney for her suggestion
that the phantom figure is the stepmother. John Seelye speculates that it
may be Ishmael's unconscious memory of his real mother (*The Ironic
Diagram*, p. 61). For some readers, the hand is "supernatural," and terror
invests the episode because it represents masturbation, a view not unlike
my own in its suggestion that Ishmael has been shamed and dissociated
from his body. The "hand" he wakes up holding does not belong to him.

6.   He who is unsure whether life is worth living loves Queequeg for
his warmth, and for bringing him back from the brink. In *Depression and
the Body*, Lowen discusses the formation, in later life, of intellectual
defenses, and the muscular contraction and emotional numbness that
result from insufficient contact, during infancy, with the mother's body.

Blau cites Ashley Montagu's observation in *Touching: The Human
Significance of the Skin* that during the nineteenth century a surprising
number of infants died of marasmus, "a Greek word meaning 'wasting
away:'

> Marasmus occurs, Montagu says, in direct relation to the
> amount and nature of tactile comfort and stimulation an
> infant receives. No wonder the literature of the period has as
> its central character the "orphan" (*The Body Impolitic*, p.
> 82).

7.

> Vindictiveness is the goal. The vindictive character does not
> experience his vindictiveness as a property of his being. He is
> possessed by it, driven by it and often harried. He literally
> cannot experience life on any other terms and he is dimly
> aware of his shortcoming although far from awareness of his
> agonizing yearning for reunion with the loved one he lost in
> the dark, forgotten past (Danields, p. 188).

Weaver says Melville was trapped in the "closet of a vindictive subcon-
scious" (*Herman Melville: Mariner and Mystic*, p. 54).

8.   Danields says that, in the end, Ahab, miming Moby-Dick,
"achieves his purpose, dying wrapped around the whale—symbolically
"welded" to it, as he said, with his own harpooneer's rope" ("Pathological
Vindictiveness," p. 193). No one has written more insightfully about the
frightful, spiteful aspects of misery in *Moby-Dick* than Thompson and
Blau, especially in the latter's discussion of the motif of "futile mimicry"
(*The Body Impolitic*, p. 88). Tolchin's reading of *Typee* addresses what
Blau calls "futile mimicry" and what I am calling vengeful fusion:

> In name Tommo pastes together the "om" and "mo" of the
> only words he teaches his Marquesan father. "H-*om*-e and

"*Mo*-ther." Through his anxious desire to resolve his grief, Tommo seems to become Maria Melville (home and mother), as he swells out the bosom of his coat with food during his escape, then later dons a petticoat, impersonates a belle, and indulges in fantasies of self-castration ...(*Mourning*, p. 57).

9. Excepting Parker and Gilman, who in his 1951 study portrays Maria as "essentially a simple, domestic, and somewhat provincial woman" (pp. 17-18), and says that "anyone who has read her letters" will find it "ludicrous" to see in them signs of the Sinister Mother, most commentators see just that. They also agree that the relationship between Maria and Herman seems not to have improved with time. Howard, citing letters of Elizabeth Shaw during the first year of her marriage to Melville, suggests that "The entire household revolved around Maria, and Elizabeth's position was that of no more than a satellite revolving around Herman..." He speaks of the mother, many years and moves later, "bombarding" Herman with suggestions for household improvements which resulted in the story "I and My Chimney" (Howard's *Herman Melville*, pp. 109, 195).
Henry Bamford Parkes writes that with Melville, as with Poe,

> sexuality is definitely conceived in immature terms, with a dominating mother-image, a strong flavor of incest, and (with Melville), an apparent element of homosexuality...("Poe, Melville and Hawthorne" in *Partisan Review*, Vol. XVI, #2, February 1949, p. 158 pp. 157-166).

10. Entrances, less than pleasant and often dangerous, frequently in Melville's works signify new, if not necessarily felicitous, beginnings. Tolchin, referring to Helen Petrullo's work on *Typee*, discusses Tommo's "amniotic perspective" (*Mourning*, p. 57).
11. This is Alice Miller's "paradise of pre-ambivalent harmony" between infant and mother—except that here the mother is male (*Drama*, p. 15). Haberstroh calls Queequeg "paternal" and notes that

> Ahab gradually comes to replace Queequeg as the focus of Ishmael's attention, a replacement that is only further evidence of Melville's uncertainties about his narrator's strengths, and Ishmael's uncertainties about himself" (*Melville and Male Identity*, pp. 14, 98).

12. It is probably clear by now that in my reading, the complicated feelings between Melville and his mother and Melville and Hawthorne, fraught with confused, angry, seductive energy, become the ambience of *Moby-Dick*, an ambience fractured in *Pierre*, which the writer evidently began in a fever as soon as he finished the proofs of *Moby-Dick*. Haberstroh suggests that Hawthorne's removal from Lenox in 1851, "seems to have been the principal cause of *Pierre*'s becoming Melville's

most undisguised expression of self-hatred (p. 104). What stands out for Haberstroh in the letter Melville wrote back to Hawthorne after receiving Hawthorne's letter, now lost, praising *Moby-Dick*, is its "distinctly hectic luster:"

> One senses here that Melville's whole mental life, along with his confidence in his capacities as an artist, hangs from the very insubstantial thread of what Melville can make himself believe Hawthorne believed about *Moby-Dick*...Melville could accept the apparently indeterminate appreciation contained in Hawthorne's letter...could make himself believe that Hawthorne was giving the great seal of artistic approval...and could rest contented in the fact that the man he imagined loved him and understood him best remained near him (*Melville and Male Identity*, pp. 106-7).

Chase remarks Hawthorne's ghostly presence in *Pierre* (Chase's *Herman Melville*, p. 113). Martin remarks Hawthorne's presence in *Clarel* (*Hero, Captain and Stranger*, pp. 14-15, 63, 102-103).

Selected Bibliography

Arvin, Newton. *Herman Melville*. London: The Viking Press, Inc., 1950.

Baird, James. *Ishmael*. Baltimore and London: The Johns Hopkins University Press, 1956.

Baym, Nina. *PMLA* 94, (1979).

——. *Novels, Readers, and Reviewers: Responses to Fiction in Antebellum America*. Ithaca and London: Cornell University Press, 1984.

Beaver, Harold. *American Critical Essays, Twentieth Century*. London: Oxford University Press, 1959.

Becker, Ernest. *The Denial of Death*. London: Collier Macmillan Publishers, 1973.

Bell, Michael Davitt. *The Development of American Romance: The Sacrifice of Relation*. Chicago and London: University of Chicago Press, 1980.

Berthoff, Warner. *The Example of Melville*. Princeton: Princeton University Press, 1962.

Blau, Richard Manley. *The Body Impolitic: A Reading of Four Novels by Herman Melville*, Costerus Series. Amsterdam: Rodopi, 1979.

Bloom, Harold, ed. *Major Literary Characters: Ahab*. New York: Chelsea House Publishers, 1991.

Boies, J.J. "The Whale Without Epilogue," *Modern Language Quarterly*, Vol. XXIV, #2, June 1963, pp. 172-177.

Braswell, William. *Melville's Religious Thought: An Essay in Interpretation*. New York: Pageant Books, 1943.

Brodhead, Richard. *Hawthorne, Melville, and the Novel*. Chicago: University of Chicago Press, 1976.

Brodtkorb, Paul. *Ishmael's White World; A Phenomenological Reading of Moby-Dick*. New Haven: Yale University Press, 1965. B

Bryant, John, ed. *A Companion to Melville Studies*. New York: Greenwood Press, 1986.

Budd, Louis J. and Cady, Edwin. H. *On Melville: The Best of American Literature*. Durham: Duke University Press, 1988.

Cameron, Sharon. *The Corporeal Self: Allegories of the Body in Melville and Hawthorne*. Baltimore and London: The Johns Hopkins University Press, 1981.

Charvat, William. *The Profession of Authorship in America, 1800-1870*. ed. Matthew J. Bruccoli. Columbus: Ohio State University Press, 1968.

Chase, Richard. *Herman Melville*. New York: The Macmillan Company, 1949.

Crews, Frederick, ed. *Psychoanalysis and Literary Process*. Cambridge, MA.: Winthrop Publishers, Inc., 1970.

Dahlberg, Edward. *Alms for Oblivion*. Minneapolis: University of Minnesota Press, 1964.

Danields, Marvin. "Pathological Vindictiveness and the Vindictive Character," *Psychoanalytic Review*, Vol. 56, #2, 1969, pp. 169-196.

DeSalvo, Louise. *Nathaniel Hawthorne*. Atlantic Highlands, New Jersey: Humanities Press International, Inc., 1987.

Dillingham, William. *Melville's Later Novels*. Athens and London: University of Georgia Press, 1986.

Dimock, Wai-chee. *Empire for Liberty: Melville and the Poetics of Individualism*. Princeton: Princeton U.P., 1989.

Dryden, Edgar. *Nathaniel Hawthorne: The Poetics of Enchantment*. Ithaca and London: Cornell University Press, 1977.

——. *Melville's Thematics of Form: The Great Art of Telling the Truth*. Baltimore: The Johns Hopkins U.P., 1968.

Edinger, Edward F. *Melville's* Moby-Dick: *A Jungian Commentary*. New York: New Directions, 1975.

Eigner, Edwin M. *The Metaphysical Novel in England and America: Dickens, Bulwer, Melville, and Hawthorne*. Berkeley, Los Angeles, and London: University of California Press, 1978.

Erikson, Erik. H. *Childhood and Society*. New York: W. W. Norton & Co., Inc., 1963.

——. *Young Man Luther*. New York: W. W. Norton and Co., Inc., 1958.

Feidelson, Charles. *Symbolism And American Literature*. Chicago: University of Chicago Press, 1953.

Fetterley, Judith. *The Resisting Reader: A Feminist Approach to American Fiction.* Bloomington and London: Indiana University Press, 1977.

Fiedler, Leslie. *Love and Death in the American Novel.* New York: Criterion Books, 1960.

———. *Partisan Review,* June 15, 1948.

———. *Nation,* November 19, 1949, pp. 494-496.

Finkelstein, Dorothee Metlitsky. *Melville's Orienda.* New York: Octagon Books, 1971.

Frazier, James. *The Golden Bough: A Study In Magic And Religion.* New York: The Macmillan Company, 1942. 1st pub. 1922.

Freedman, Ralph. *The Lyrical Novel.* Princeton: Princeton U.P., 1971.

Friedman, Alan. *The Turn of the Novel.* London: Oxford U.P., 1966.

Gay, Peter. "Blame Wagner." *Vogue.* Feb. 1983: 302-304, 345-348, from "The Impossibility of Innocence," Unpublished essay. Department of History, Yale University.

Geist, Stanley. *Herman Melville.* New York: Octagon Books, 1966.

Gilman, William H. *Melville's Early Life and Redburn.* New York: New York U.P., 1951.

Gilmore, Michael T., ed. *Twentieth-Century Interpretations of Moby-Dick.* Englewood Cliffs: Prentice-Hall, Inc., 1977.

Graves, Robert. *The Greek Myths.* Volume One. Baltimore: Penguin Books, Inc, 1968. 1st pub. 1955.

Haberstroh, Charles J. Jr. *Melville and Male Identity.* Cranbury, N.J.: Associated University Press, 1980.

Hawthorne, Nathaniel. *The House of the Seven Gables.* Boston and New York: Houghton Mifflin Co., 1952. 1st pub. 1851.

Hegel, G. W. F. *The Phenomenology of Mind.* Trans. J. B. Baillie. Harper and Row: New York, 1967. 1st. pub. 1807.

Herbert, T. Walter, Jr. Moby-Dick *and Calvinism.* New Brunswick: Rutgers University Press, 1977.

Hetherington, Hugh W. *Melville's Reviewers, British and American, 1846-1891.* Chapel Hill: University of North Carolina Press, 1961.

Higgins, Brian and Parker, Herschel, eds. *Critical Essays on Herman Melville's* Moby-Dick. New York: Macmillan Publishing Co., 1992.

Hillway, Tyrus. *Herman Melville.* New York: Twayne Publishers, Inc., 1963

———. and Mansfield, Luther S., eds. Moby-Dick: *Centennial Essays.* Dallas: Southern Methodist University Press, 1953.

Howard, Leon. *Herman Melville.* Berkeley: University of California Press, 1951.

Iser, Wolfgang. *The Act of Reading: A Theory of Aesthetic Response.* Baltimore and London: The Johns Hopkins University Press, 1978.

James, C.L.R. *Mariners, Renegades and Castaways: The Story of Herman Melville and the World We Live In.* Detroit: Bewick/Ed, 1978. 1st. pub. 1953.

Kazin, Alfred. *New Republic*, Dec. 18, 1944.

———. *The New Yorker.* February 12, 1949.

Kierkegaard, Soren. *A Kierkegaard Anthology.* New York: The Modern Library, 1946.

Kitto, H. D.F. *The Greeks.* London: Penguin Books, Inc., 1981. lst pub. 1957.

———. *Greek Tragedy: A Literary Study.* London: Methuen & Co., 1939.

Klein, Melanie. *Our Adult World and Other Essays.* New York: Basic Books, 1963.

Kristeva, Julia. *Powers of Horror: An Essay on Abjection.* Trans. Leon S. Roudiez. New York: Columbia University Press, 1982.

Lacan, Jacques. *Four Fundamental Concepts of Psychoanalysis.* New York: Norton, 1978.

Lamb, Charles. *The Complete Works and Letters of Charles Lamb.* New York: The Modern Library, 1935.

Lange, John Peter, ed., *A Commentary on the Holy Scriptures.* New York: Charles Scribner's Sons, 1893.

Lasch, Christopher. *The Culture of Narcissism: American Life in an Age of Diminishing Expectations.* New York: W. W. Norton and Co., Inc., 1978.

Lawrence, D. H. *Studies in Classic American Literature.* Garden City, New York: Doubleday & Co., Inc. 1951. lst pub. 1923.

Lee, A. Robert, ed. *Herman Melville: Reassessments.* London: Vision and Barnes and Noble, 1984.

Levin, Harry. *The Power of Blackness.* Chicago: Ohio University Press, 1958.

Levine, Robert. S., ed. *The Cambridge Companion to Herman Melville.*Cambridge, U.K.: Cambridge U.P., 1998.

Leyda, Jay. *The Melville Log.* New York: Harcourt, Brace and Company, 1951.

Lowen, Alexander. *Depression and the Body: The Biological Basis of Faith and Reality.* New York: Penguin Books, 1983. 1st pub. 1972.

———. *Narcissism: Denial of the True Self.* New York: Macmillan Publishing Co., Inc., 1983.

Martin, Robert K. *Hero, Captain, and Stranger: Male Friendship, Social Critique, and Literary Form in the Sea Novels of Herman Melville.* Chapel Hill and London: The University of North Carolina Press, 1986.

Matthieson, F.O. *American Renaissance: Art and Expression in the Age of Emerson and Whitman.* London and New York: Oxford U.P., 1949.

Mengeling, Marvin E. "The Fundamental Principles," *Emerson Society Quarterly* 38, First Quarter, 1965. pp. 74-87

Melville, Herman. *Moby-Dick* ed. Harrison Hayford and Hershel Parker. New York: W. W. Norton & Co., Inc., 1967. 1st pub. 1851.

Metcalf, Eleanor Melville. *Herman Melville: Cycle and Epicycle.* Cambridge: Harvard University Press, 1953.

Miller, Alice. *The Drama of the Gifted Child: How Narcissistic Parents Form and Deform the Emotional Lives of Their Gifted Children.* (Originally published as *Prisoners of Childhood*). Trans. Ruth Ward. New York: Basic Books, 1981.

——. *For Your Own Good: Hidden Cruelty in Child-Rearing and the Roots of Violence.* Trans. Hildegarde and Hunter Hannun. New York: Farrar, Straus, and Giroux, Inc.,1983.

Miller, Edwin Haviland. *Melville.* New York: George Braziller, 1975.

Miller, Perry. *The New England Mind: From Colony to Province.* Cambridge: Harvard University Press, 1953.

——. *The New England Mind: The Seventeenth Century.* New York: Macmillan Publishing Co., Inc., 1939. and Thomas H. Johnson, eds.

——. *The Puritans.* New York: Harper and Row Publishers, Inc., 1963.

Mumford, Lewis. *Herman Melville.* New York: Harcourt, Brace and Company, 1929.

Murray, Henry A. "In Nomine Diaboli". *New England Quarterly* 24 (1951): 432-52.

——. Introduction. *Pierre, or the Ambiguities.* New York: Hendricks House, 1949.

Olson, Charles. *Call Me Ishmael: A Study of Melville.* San Francisco: City Light Books, 1947.

Parker, Hershel. *Herman Melville: A Biography.* Baltimore: Johns Hopkins U.P., 1996.

Parker, Hershel and Hayford, Harrison. Moby-Dick *as Doubloon: Essays and Extracts, (1851-1970).* New York: W. W. Norton and Co., Inc., 1970.

Parkes, Henry Bamford. "Poe, Melville and Hawthorne: An Essay in Sociological Criticism," *Partisan Review*, Vol. XVI, #2, February, 1949, pp. 157-166.

Parrington, Vernon Louis. *Main Currents in American Thought: An Interpretation of American Literature From the Beginnings to 1920.* New York: Harcourt, Brace Jovanovich, Inc., 1930.

Pease, Donald. "Moby-Dick and the Cold War," *The American Renaissance Reconsidered*. Baltimore and London: The Johns Hopkins U.P., 1985.

Peck, Scott. *People of the Lie: The Hope for Healing Human Evil*. New York: Simon and Schuster, Inc. 1983.

Pommer, Henry F. *Milton and Melville*. Pittsburgh: University of Pittsburgh Press, 1950.

Porter, Carolyn. "Call Me Ishmael, or How to Make Double-Talk Speak," *New Essays on* Moby-Dick. Cambridge,U.K.: Cambridge U.P., 1986.

Pullin, Faith, ed. *New Perspectives on Melville*. Kent, Ohio: The Kent State University Press, 1978.

Renker, Elizabeth. *Strike Through the Mask: Herman Melville and the Scene of Writing*. Baltimore: Johns Hopkins U.P., 1996.

Robertson-Lorant, Laurie. *Melville: A Biography*. New York: Clarkson Potter Publishers, 1996.

Rich, Adrienne. *Dark Fields of the Republic: Poems 1991-1995*. New York: W. W. Norton, 1995.

Rogin, Michael Paul. *Subversive Genealogies: The Politics and Art of Herman Melville*. New York: Alfred A. Knopf, 1983.

Rothschild, H. Jr., "The Language of Mesmerism in *Moby-Dick*," *English Studies*, Vol. 53, #3, June 1972.

Rountree, Thomas J., ed. *Critics on Melville: Readings in Literary Criticism*. Coral Gables, Florida: University of Miami Press, 1972.

Sealts, Merton M., Jr. *The Early Lives of Melville: Nineteenth Century Biographical Sketches and Their Authors*. Madison: University of Wisconsin Press, 1974.

Sedgwick, William Ellery. *Herman Melville: The Tragedy of Mind*. New York: Russell and Russell, 1962.

Seelye, John. *The Ironic Diagram*. Evanston: Northwestern University Press, 1970.

Stern, Milton R. *The Fine-Hammered Steel of Herman Melville*. Urbana: University of Illinois Press, 1957.

Stone, Geoffrey. *Melville*. New York: Sheed and Ward, 1949.

Sulieman, Susan R., and Inge Crosman, eds. *The Reader In the Text: Essays on Audience and Interpretation*. Princeton: Princeton University Press, 1980.

Thompson, Lawrance. *Melville's Quarrel With God*. Princeton: Princeton University Press, 1952.

Tolchin, Neal L. *Mourning, Gender and Creativity in the Art of Herman Melville*. New Haven: Yale University Press, 1988.

Tompkins, Jane. *Reader-Response Criticism*. Baltimore and London: The Johns Hopkins University Press, 1980.

Updike, John. *The New Yorker*. May 10, 1982.

Weaver, Raymond. *Herman Melville: Mariner and Mystic*. New York: Cooper Square Publishers, Inc., 1968. lst pub. 1921.

Weiskel, Thomas. *The Romantic Sublime: Studies in the Structure and Psychology of Transcendence*. Baltimore and London: The Johns Hopkins University Press, 1976.

Widmer, Kingsley. *The Ways of Nihilism: A Study of Herman Melville's Short Novels*. Los Angeles: The California State Colleges, 1970.

Wilson, W. Daniel. *PMLA 96*, 1981.

Winnicott, D. W. *The Child and the Outside World: Studies in Developing Relationships*. London: Tavistock Publications Ltd., 1957.

Woodson, Thomas. "Ahab's Greatness: Prometheus as Narcissus," *Journal of English Literary History*, 33, September, 1966.

Wolf, Bryan Jay. *Romantic Re-Vision: Culture and Consciousness in Nineteenth-Century American Painting and Literature*. Chicago and London: University of Chicago Press, 1982.

Wright, Nathalie. "Moby-Dick: Jonah's or Job's Whale?" *American Literature: A Journal of Literature, Criticism and Bibliography*, Vol. XXXVII, May, 1965, pp. 190-195.

Zoellner, Robert. *The Salt-Sea Mastadon: A Reading of Moby-Dick*. Berkeley, Los Angeles, and London: University of California Press, 1973.

Index

unseeing eyes, xviii, 8, 10, 66,
      69

vengeance, 8, 39, 55, 69, 83